Love Mom

Becoming
THE JOURNEY TO LOVE

Becoming Books LLC.

Becoming
THE JOURNEY TO LOVE

Edited by **Dr. Joan Samuels-Dennis** PH.D

© 2020 by Joan Samuels-Dennis

All rights reserved. No part of this book may be reproduced, stored in a retrieval system, or transmitted in any form or by any means, including electronic and mechanical photocopy, recording, scanning, or other – except for brief quotations in critical reviews or articles, without the prior written permission of the publisher.

Published in Toronto, Ontario, by Becoming Books LLC, a subsidiary of Becoming Canada Inc.

Scripture quotations marked (AMP) are taken from the Amplified Bible, Copyright © 1954, 1958, 1962, 1964, 1965, 1987 by The Lockman Foundation. Used by permission.

Scripture quotations marked (NLT) taken from the Holy Bible, New Living Translation, copyright © 1996, 2004, 2007, 2013 by Tyndale House Foundation. Used by permission of Tyndale House Publishers, Inc., Carol Stream, Illinois 60188. All rights reserved.

Scripture quotations marked (MSG) are taken from THE MESSAGE, copyright © 1993, 1994, 1995, 1996, 2000, 2001, 2002 by Eugene H. Peterson. Used by permission of NavPress. All rights reserved. Represented by Tyndale House Publishers, Inc.

ISBN: 978-1-9994861-7-4

This book is dedicated to all the women in the world who have endured racism, colourism, sexism, classism, micro-aggression, social exclusion, genocide, spiritual terrorization and now desire to bring peace into their life. We celebrate the living testimony of the women who have suffered physical, emotional and sexual violence and through it all say with a loud voice, "my help comes from the Lord, the maker of heaven and earth!"

Contents

1. The Village of Peace • 1
2. The Voice • 19
3. Sometimes Coffee, Sometimes Tea • 55
4. Center Stage • 79
5. The Return Home • 99
6. Pain To Purpose • 119
7. Broken But Not Defeated • 145
8. I Choose To Love • 179
9. High Up, Fallen, Back Up • 199
10. Mama and Me • 217
11. The Cry of The Children • 247
12. Undercurrents Within • 269
13. Dreams That Awaken • 297
14. Christ-Like Forgiveness • 311
15. Becoming • 323
16. Dr. Joan • 331

CHAPTER 1

The Village of Peace

I AM Joan Samuels-Dennis

> Joel 2:28 (AMP)
> *"It shall come about after this*
> *That I shall pour out My Spirit on all mankind;*
> *And your sons and your daughters will prophesy,*
> *Your old men will dream dreams,*
> *Your young men will see visions."*

Even in childhood, I had fantastic dreams that played like a movie. Over the years as I shared my dreams, I came to realize that no one I had ever known, spoke of similar experiences. In 2016, I moved from having vivid dreams to experiencing visions — a spiritual encounter that unfolds like a movie while I am fully conscious. The shift occurred at the moment of my spiritual awakening.

A belief or faith in God is different from awakening. Many religious people, including Christians, hold the view that they are fully awake and conscious of who God is, when in fact they are still sleeping. *Faith* is being sure that what we hope for will be manifested, and being convinced of the existence of things we cannot see (Hebrews 11:1 [AMP]). *Awakening* is the opening of our spiritual eyes and an expansion of the consciousness that allows us to see, touch and communicate with a God in whom we believe, trust and hope. I do not speak of a one-sided communication in which we talk, God listens, and somehow we sense or perceive his response. I mean a real, in-person interaction and a purposeful conversation that directs our path.

Two forces converged between 2015 and 2016 to open my spiritual eyes and initiate my spiritual transformation. In 2015, I embarked on a healing journey that made forgiveness front and centre of the process. I don't mean forget the wrong; this forgiveness process asks instead that you remember every detail of the event. I don't mean let go of the negative emotions and move on; this style of forgiveness asks instead that you become conscious of the triggers of fear embedded in every moment or interaction you forgive. I don't mean reconcile; this style of forgiveness asks instead that you discern who is good and capable of have loving and authentic connections.

This style of forgiveness is grounded in the science of mirror neurons. Brain cells called mirror neurons allow us to step into the consciousness of another during loving and unloving moments. As we experience an event through the eyes of another, we assume their thoughts, speech and behaviours. If we experience love, we mirror love. If we experience fear, we mirror fear. Our most painful moments dictate our behavioural responses until we look intently at them and ask four questions:

1. What did I want from the person(s) in that moment?

2. What did I get instead?

3. How did I feel in that moment?

4. What fear was poured into their life that they now pour into mine?

Christ asks each of us to end the judgement, criticism and condemnation of one another because he understood that each of us are repeating generational and life patterns grounded in an unconscious fear response. These fear responses are permanently broken as we stand in front of a mirror, face the person who wronged us and ask the four questions noted above. An amazing thing happens as we move through the forgiveness process: we develop Christ-like compassionate understanding. Beyond this, we see the ways in which we have harmed ourselves and others in the same way we were harmed. As we move through the forgiveness process, we release the one with the speck of dust in their eye and ask God to forgive our blindness to the fear-based patterns we have been repeating. True repentance comes as we make the decision to love the one who wronged us, accept the circumstance and break the chain of fear embedded in that moment. Our eyes become filled with light as we make the decision to live and love like Christ.

Forgiveness is now intimately woven into every delicate detail of my daily life. I have forgiven my mother and father, my three sisters and brother, and members of my extended family for deep wounds of betrayal and violence. I have forgiven co-workers, bosses and authority figures for refusing to see me, my gifts and my talents. I have forgiven people of European descent for being unjust, discriminatory, oppressive, exclusionary and inhumane. I have forgiven the on-looker nations — those who watched silently as my people struggled and died and our children suffocated. I have forgiven women for their unkindness and speaking hateful words in the heart, soul and mind of men and children. I have forgiven men for violating women and children and for fighting unnecessary wars grounded and fortified in fear. Like Christ, I have forgiven Adam and Eve, my ancestors and all humanity for being a *stiff-necked disobedient people.*

After moving through my own forgiveness journey, my dreams shifted into visions. Today, I use both my dreams and visions to share spiritual wisdom or knowledge that can be used to inspire growth, enlightenment and transformation among God's people. Not long ago, I had a dream that allowed me to come to a full understanding of the path we must all travel to fully embrace peace in our lives. The dream announced my arrival into the place I call the *village of peace.*

The dream begins on the shores of Africa. I stand with two men on a beautiful but narrow shoreline and I take in the beauty of the scenery. Though I am in Africa, the place reminds me of the Caribbean. The beach sits below a massive and ever-expanding mountain, the heights of which would compare to a 100-story building. The face of the mountain is rough and strong. The light clay-coloured contours of the mountain shimmer in the backdrop of the perfectly blue sky. The top of this mountain is adorned by rolling hills with green carpet-like grass.

I stand at the base of this mountain with two white men dressed as sailors. Their outfit is something from another time. Cream coloured shorts, with a delicately designed shirt. White shoes and socks that come to a point just below their knee.

"I am going to find my friend Amenze," I say to the two white men.

The expression on one of the men's face catches my attention. It was as though he was saying, "Why would you go searching for her now?"

But, without any further discussion, I head off down the beach. Though there is no path up this massive mountain, I look for a place to begin my climb. Not long after starting my climb, something from deep in my spirit tells me to look out at the ocean and it is then that the quizzical look on the man's faces makes sense. Way off in the distance is a massive wave. A tsunami the height of the mountain I now climb. My heart jumps and begins to race. At that moment I am faced with a decision. Do I turn back or continue? I look out at the wave one more time and I notice something. The wave is moving slowly; slow like a turtle. I have all the time I need to get to the top of this mountain. So I redecide: "I am going to find my friend Amenze!"

My decision sends a signal to the God of the Universe. As I continue my climb, a path avails itself. The path is small but worn. Many have gone before me. Young trees spread out on both sides and like the top of the massive mountain, the grass is the purest shade of green. Time means nothing in this place. I walk the path and soon come to the entrance of a village. As I enter the village I notice it is completely shrouded in tall, majestic trees that offer a refreshing shade. The ground is not grass, but rich black soil. In this village, life is simple. The villagers are black women who live in tiny houses that sit on stilts.

There is a Godly character that emanates from these women. They are strong, wise, kind and pure. A woman with beautiful black skin passes me as I make my way to the highest point in the village. It is not the fruit basket on her head that catches my attention, but how her dark skin resembles the beautiful soil on which she walks. As she passes me, she gives me a warm and welcoming smile. Another woman sits at the entrance of her home and says hello with a wide smile expressed only by her beautiful eyes.

Peace.

Peace.

There is only peace in this place.

I eventually make my way to the centre of the village and I begin to ask the women gathered there if they know where I can find Amenze.

"Amenze doesn't live here dear," one woman says to me. "She lives in a village a good distance from here."

She notices I am contemplating the thought of continuing the journey and immediately intervenes. "You won't be able to travel any further today," she announces. "You better settle in with us. The wave is coming."

She welcomes me in and though we are four in her tiny house, there is more than enough room for me, her and her two children. I am aware that her son is the only male in the entire village. In this tiny home is a small kitchen, a bedroom and a living room. The place is meticulously decorated. Humility decorates hers, and I suspect, all other homes in this village. An ambience of grace and mercy fills the air. We chat together for hours while the wave slowly moves in and overtakes the village. Its presence is fully known when the house lifts off its stilts and begins to rock like a boat on water. Though the water should come in through the floorboards, the floor remains completely dry.

From the living room, I look out a large window and the awesomeness of the view humbles me. The great wave has covered everything. Like the days of Noah, the earth is covered. For the first time, my thoughts return to the two men on the beach. "How did they survive the massive wave?" I wonder. It is then I remember the clipboard with the passenger manifest one man held in his hand. These men were sailors and they survived daily by going out in their ships.

Time passes as I watch the tsunami become a river under my feet.

My friend Amenze now sits on a chair in the small living room where I stood consumed by the awesomeness of the wave. Born in Nigeria, her name means river water, peaceful. *Peaceful water* sits and talks with me. Her skin is black and beautiful like all the other women in this village. My peace is complete with her presence. She is not mesmerized by the wave like I am. She has had a busy day and she passes on a nugget of wisdom just before I wake. That day her task was to make a presentation to a group of people in another village, but she had shown up late for some reason she did not reveal. As she recounted the events of the day, she recalled the scolding of a young man named Abe. "That was a good presentation," he said with a disapproving tone, "but you need to show up on time. The people here are relying on us and it's important that you organize yourself and show up on time."

Even in the midst of his reprimand, in a state of complete peace, I wake.

I have learned so much from this dream. The village of peace is real and finding it is a choice.

The people who have been born to bring peace into our world are the ones who have endured the war and the aftereffects of cultural violence and annihilation. The women who have endured racism, colourism, sexism, classism, micro-aggression and social exclusion, but now desire to bring peace back into their lives. The one who has suffered physical, emotional and sexual violence and through it all has been able to say, "my help comes from the Lord, the maker of heaven and earth."

Sometimes when we tell people about the plans we have for our personal life, our marriage or relationships, our children, our business and even our frame of mind, they give us a strange quizzical look. It's almost like they're saying "Are you serious?"

Because they don't know what you're truly searching for, they don't understand your tactics either. So they ask you questions like: "Are you sure this is the right time?"

It is so tempting to try to convince them to see where you're coming from and where you're going, but if you're serious you won't get caught up in all of that. When you know with confidence what your intentions are, their quizzical looks will not matter. You simply take notice and move on.

The sailors on that beach were challenging. "Peace? What do you mean you are going in search of peace right now?" Have you ever thought about your desire to change careers, your new business start-up, your decision to end the violent marriage or toxic relationship, or seeking counselling as your way of searching for peace? How many times as you stepped out in pursuit of something meaningful did someone say:

"The conditions aren't right."

"But you have never done this before."

"There is a massive wave coming your direction and how will you survive?"

"Settle down, don't get excited. Just stay in your state of restlessness."

Rather than support you in finding peace they would rather you stay where you have always been—the nagging normal of conflict, stuckness, despair.

The same people will go to the length of with-holding necessary information as they tell you the lie that war is normal and peace is unattainable or out of your reach. We must express the desire to seek peace and even after you see everyone else's doubts, you step out and hold firm to your decision. You have to raise your voice and let the God of the universe know *"I am stepping out. I want to live my destiny…I will build that Empire. I want peace. I am serious!"*

Once we commit to the journey, each of us is required to be mindful. The Merriam-Webster dictionary defines mindfulness as the quality or state of being conscious or aware of something. It is also defined as a mental state achieved by focussing one's awareness on the present moment, while calmly acknowledging and accepting one's feelings, thoughts and bodily sensations. Mindfulness has become a very popular therapeutic technique and I teach it to my clients all the time. But the most mindful people are those who connect deeply with the spirit within.

Let me return to Joel 2:28 for a moment. *"It shall come about after this that I shall pour out My Spirit on all mankind."* The spirit of God is in all of us. When we are mindful, we're connected with our spirit and with God's spirit. When we are mindful, we have a universal understanding of what the wave is.

What does the tsunami represent?

The tsunami represents chaos, our greatest fears, the things that overwhelm and cover us. But the tsunami is not what kills us, it's our unwillingness and our inability to rise — our inability to go up the mountain and become the very image of God.

It's not racism that kills our potential, but our lack of identity and poor race esteem — how good we feel about being a member of the HUMAN race without all the categorizations that create false pride. We are children of a living God and yet too few of us deeply connect with this truth. When we are mindful, we know who we are, and no one can tell us what we should look like, sound like, be like.

In my book *490: Forgive and Live Fearlessly*, I introduce the 7-step forgiveness process I call Christ-like forgiveness. I believe this style of forgiveness is the most profound and effective way of becoming mindful. It shows us the deep-rooted lies connected to the false self — the *wounded* self — and the self that searches for things in the world to help us deal with those wounds. This term is used with slight variations by authors like Thomas Keating, Thomas Merton and Richard Rohr. For Keating, the false self is created when we experience an event that then causes a trauma-response. It sustains a false but overwhelming need for power and/or control, esteem and/or affection, and security and/or survival. We develop fear-based *attachments* to people, places and situations that bring us a false sense of safety. Alternatively, we also develop fear-based *aversions* to people, places and situations that mirror the circumstance in which we were wounded.

Forgiveness exposes the false self and the lies we believe about ourselves, others and God. It shows us how fear forces us to live in the shadows, diminishes our potential, limits where we go and the things we do. Mindful people know their truth, speak truth and can quickly discern when others are speaking from the perspective of the true or false self. Mindful people know their wounds and the fears those wounds created. They do not freeze in the midst of fear but instead, act with decisiveness, grace and authority.

The wave comes every single day, and neither you nor I can stop it. The important thing to do is move! You cannot get stuck looking at the wave. Set your goals, always ensure that you embed them in your greater purpose and every day ask yourself this question: "What is the one brave and bold thing I can do today to let God know I am serious about rising to a height where this wave cannot touch me?" Then do it!

As you act remain rooted and grounded in the ever-expanding light, love and peace of the Holy Spirit. In November of 2016, one month after the vision of this book was formed in my mind, I embarked on a 21-day journey to China. It was a spiritual retreat, but not of the sort you might imagine. My mother-in-law and I went to China to care for my husband who had experienced a massive stroke after disembarking from his plane at the Shanghai airport. Shortly after returning from China, I had two interconnected visions about three months apart. In the vision I now call RISE, God showed me a spiritual transformation map that took me three years to navigate. In a second vision, my purpose was clarified and a staff — the message of spiritual transformation — was placed in my hand.

I have discovered something hidden in scriptures since the original texts were written: eternal life is not granted to everyone who believes in Christ. Rather, it is granted to those who believe and transform into the very image of Christ. Revelations 12:11 talks about those who overcome in this way: "…and they overcame and conquered him because of the blood of the Lamb and because of the word of their testimony, for they did not love their life and renounce their faith even when faced with death." The wave is a tremendous force and there are three choices available to all humanity as we notice the chaos, pain and overwhelm that comes with seeing the wave: First, some of us choose to die. We say out loud, "This is all too much. If this is what life is like, I choose not to live it." Second, we birth the false self and feed its insatiable need for power, affection and security. We rely on human ingenuity, personal advantage, the building of boats, monitoring systems and charting a tumultuous course that ensures we live through another day. A final group will see the wave for what it is—the creation of a living testimony and the opportunity to rise even when faced with certain death.

Though many believe in Christ, it is a maturing faith and expanding hope that prompts us to seek peace. It is the desire for peace that inspires us to embark on the difficult journey that comes with practicing Christ-like forgiveness. We forgive every known and unknown individual, group, community, institution, country, nation and humanity for creating the fears that inspire the creation of the false self.

Looking across all acts of forgiveness, we begin to notice a pattern. Each forgiveness reveals a list of wants or spiritual desires that when combined allows us to speak our love language—the unique way we desire to give and receive love. There are variations in how we define love, but each of us is seeking compassion, gracious favour that is unconditional, patience, kindness, commitment, truth and faithfulness. This perfect love we desire is possessed only by God. It is only when we overcome the fears birthed by our wounds that we realize the love we seek has always been present.

Spiritual baptism which allows for the full operation of the Holy Spirit in our lives eventually leads to the death of the false self and finally reveals the part of ourselves that always was—the *true self*. *Oneness* is a powerful part of the transformation journey characterized by the true self becoming one with the spirit of life. It is here that we overcome fear, sin and death. As the journey continues the spiritual gifts are released and like trees planted by living water, the fruits of the Holy Spirit bloom. It is then, and only then that we have the *word of our testimony*. In the final stage of the transformation process, the Holy Spirit empowers us to live our God-given mission. Daily, we go down to the beach and for those who are ready, we now act as guides.

There is a way of being that is represented by the black woman. Sometimes I call it *spiritual transformation*. Sometimes *Rising*. But I also take notice of the colour of the woman's skin and the connection to the earth beneath her feet and sometimes I choose to call this process *Becoming Beautiful I am*. The journey, whatever we call it, allows us to rest in peace at the top of a great mountain that breaks the destructive force of the wave. That tower of refuge can only be called God.

Once we decide to pursue peace, God creates new life-giving pathways that make the journey refreshing and easy. The journey makes us spiritually calm and the blessings of God's favour flow life-giving joy into each of our hearts. We enter countless villages of peace with sisters who mirror the very character of God. We take up our spiritual position as peacemakers. Twenty-four hours a day we possess within our spirit an eternal knowing: the wave comes every day. But at these heights, only peaceful waters flow.

CHAPTER 2

The Voice

I AM Kate Kelty

There was a chill in the air and the crunch of autumn under my little five-year-old feet. The wooded path carried my mama and me to this promised date I'd begged and longed for. It was our time — our breakfast picnic in the woods that graced the edge of our cul-de-sac. This forest offered daily adventure and a match to my imagination. Our picnic had been long anticipated. The youngest of three children, I was always eager for any one-on-one time with my mom. It was also a chance to run away with the only person who I felt understood me and liked me.

My hair was neatly braided into two pigtails, and if I closed my eyes tight and imagined my brown hair was red, I was at once Anne Shirley, my favourite literary hero. She was much more than a girl in a book to me. She was all spunk and spirit and made me feel like I wasn't alone in the world. I wasn't the only one who got in trouble and who exasperated those around her with her wild imaginings, unequalled curiosity and red-hot temper. If only the leaves falling to the ground were from sprawling trees in the forest of Avonlea and not a cul-de-sac off of Boulder Brook Drive in the suburbs of Atlanta Georgia. When I was with Anne, I didn't feel all alone in being "bad." There was even a hint that her type of "bad" could be beautiful. To use Anne's words, we were definitely "kindred spirits." The only other person in my world who made me feel safe in my skin was my mama. This breakfast date was a chance to revel in that.

Most of the time I ventured into the woods accompanied by my older siblings, who were almost always a little irritated at their baby sister who tagged along. But this day was different. There was something magical about entering the woods and being the only child in my mother's care, free to be the Katie that twirled and sang at the top of her lungs. Free to move this way and that within the sun's invitation, to shine in the joyful watch and wonder of my mother's eye. Even now I can see her delight in my uncontained and unmeasured "Katie-ness." When I was with mama, I could almost believe I was special.

Voice The Kidnapper

As far back as I can remember, I was a problem. I couldn't have been more different from my older brother and sister, who were always cooperative — always a sweet delight. My mom tells me now that I made everyone laugh and that I was a joy, but my memories are distorted and harness a sense of disappointment. I was a disappointment. I was an irritation. I was "too much." A controlling squeeze from my sister, a jarring laugh from my brother, a "go to your room" from my dad. In this particular scene — just mama and me in the woods — I was protected from all of that. I was protected from the pain of others' disapproval of me and the sadness that came from feeling inadequate. On our breakfast date, I felt the reassurance of her joy in me. For a brief moment, I felt it all so completely, and the experience of being loved and accepted was wonderful. But the joy of this moment would be short-lived because just as we began our walk home, *he* came. He always came. My kidnapper.

I remember seeing the faces of children on the grocery store wall and learning for the first time what "kidnapped" meant. Our family came up with a code phrase to use if anyone other than mom and dad approached us. Somehow, we came up with "dirty diapers, bruises and bumps," something silly perhaps to lighten the heaviness of the conversation. I wish my kidnapper had been a physical being. I would have asked him the code word and ran for dear life . . . but this was a kidnapper of the heart.

It was as if he stood in the shadows, waiting for those moments when he saw that I was happy and unhindered. He never allowed me to forget "who I really was." He was good at his job, always branding and rebranding his scarlet letter upon my tiny soul. I didn't know at the age of five who this kidnapper was, just that in his presence I wanted to run away from myself. Whenever he came, I was consumed with what I now know to be shame, guilt and fear. I began to think of him as "B" for at the age of five, life was either good ("G") or bad ("B"). As an adult, I have been able to unmask this kidnapper and see him for who he really is — a robber, killer and destroyer of love, joy, peace and hope. Deception is his name. How does a little girl come to know an enemy such as this? How does a little girl fall prey to such vicious lies at such a tender age? Abuse does this to a child. It is a constant voice usurping the innocence and joy of being. A constant reminder that in every sun-drenched moment, there is a shadow and in that shadow darkness has a claim on the soul of its victim. I couldn't make it go away. I couldn't anticipate when he would come. I could only brace myself, shut my eyes tight and wait for "B" to leave me alone, for at least a little while. It was pure evil that he ransacked my perfect morning in the woods with mama. I didn't dance back from the woods that day. My spunk was gone. I grew quiet. I hung my head in shame, remembering, and wished I was someone else.

The memories of my sexual abuse are vague. Perhaps worse are the thoughts and images that were born in the aftermath — both evil and disturbing. It was a few years before I shared what happened down the street at the neighbour's house, but even then, it was vague. It happened at the hands of another child, a girl, not that much older than me. Perhaps she was being molested by someone else and was acting out her own pain, pleasure and confusion. The details escape me, but the shame and fear has lasted a lifetime. A door was opened to a dangerous sexual realm and evil thoughts tormented me. How does one capture the villain of the mind? This enemy lived in my imagination (or perhaps my subconscious), where knives were used to molest little girls and church sanctuaries lined with coffins instead of pews were whorehouses. I am still painfully perplexed at how these images and thoughts could originate in a mind still innocent in so many ways. Was I exposed to pornography? Something satanic? Was an even greater abuse perhaps repressed? How could it be abuse if it was happening with another child? How could it be abuse if I continued to accept invitations to go and play? In time I began to share with my mom, both the memories of my abuse and my dark, obsessive thoughts. With no framework for this type of violation, I think my mom assumed this was curious child's play. She sought to comfort me, instructing me that "I was OK" and I didn't have to share every obsessive thought with her. She meant to calm me, but I interpreted her instruction as meaning my situation was too dark for even my mom to handle. I was repulsive.

I had asked my mom not to tell my dad what had happened at the neighbour's house, but I was so young, and it was only right that she share with him. I didn't know he knew anything until he took me to a new friend's house to play and I was strongly chided not to "hurt" this little girl. My kidnapper struck a match against this strip of rough words and gleefully tossed it on the fragile kindling of my heart. A fire quickly ripped through me, flames erupting in the oily lie that I was a villain, not a victim. I was frozen and speechless staring back at my daddy. All my six-year-old eyes could understand was that he was afraid of me.

I went inside to spend the day and night with my new friend Laura. We had a wonderful time laughing and playing, but when bedtime came, the pain and fear I had been able to ignore from earlier that day with my dad came back with a vengeance. I distinctly remember falling asleep that night to the deceiver's wicked song and a whole new level of self-hatred, fear and shame ensued. It is very important that I write here that my mom and dad are not the enemies of my childhood. They loved and parented as best they were able based on their interpretation of my limited understanding and ability to communicate. Any mistakes they made have been forgiven through a heart of understanding and compassion for how and who they were in 1986. There is one enemy, the deceiver of the heart, and he will take anything he can use to twist love into hate . . . especially the words and deeds of a father. For this I grieve.

Mama's Voice

At the age of seven, we moved from Georgia to Virginia, and I continued to try to find myself amid the shackles of my memories, and the pain of guilt and shame. I was still a spirited, vibrant little girl, but there was a very fuzzy line between my fears and reality. I remember making new friends and coming home from play dates fearing that I had hurt them. Even now as I write, I feel my heart melting inside me at the thought. Of course, none of this had happened, but I hated and feared myself so much that I couldn't tell the difference between the lies and the truth. The years went by, and I continued to struggle deeply with self-hatred. Of course, sweet mama was always present with her steadiness and faithfulness in love and truth.

There was one day in elementary when a school friend was taunting and mean to me. I came home in tears. My mother sat me down in a chair next to her at the dining room table. She held a long legal pad of yellow lined paper and began to write the alphabet down the left-hand side. Then she proceeded to speak and write simultaneously:

"A is for Adorable. Katie is adorable."

"B is for Bold. Katie is bold."

"C is for Creative. Katie is creative."

On and on she went from A to Z, lifting my heart from

the ground and giving new and real meaning to who I was. I didn't realize it at the time, but my mom wasn't just complimenting me. My mom was telling me the truth, the only weapon against the deceiver. My mom's voice of truth was powerful that day. Perhaps I wasn't a mistake. Perhaps I was loveable. But my mom couldn't be the voice in my head, and eventually, the lies grew louder than the truth and messages of my worthlessness returned. I would look at my older sister and long for her perfection and long for the uncomplicated relationship she had with our dad. He never fussed at her. She never gave anyone any reason to do anything but admire her. I will never forget the day I ran out of the house in tears. I can't remember the reason now, but running away seemed like my only option. I ran all the way to the nearest gas station, but when I got there, I realized the problem had "run away" with me. I couldn't go home and have anything ever get better unless I didn't bring the problem with me. I thought of my perfect, beautiful big sister and all the way home I chanted, "I will be Kristen. I will be Kristen." It is a painful memory — the day I put a voice to the self-hatred I carried. The day I acknowledged aloud that I wished I'd been born someone else.

I carried the lies with me everywhere I went. But no matter how hard I tried to be perfect — to act like Kristen — I was still Katie. Like the time I called my Grade 4 principal by his first name on a dare in the lunchroom. Only two other children heard me. I could tell by the look on his face that he was steaming mad. I immediately gushed an apology, but the damage had been done. The guard dogs within him had been unleashed and they were coming for me. He yelled loud, "GET IN MY OFFICE NOW!" It was so loud that he set off the cafeteria siren which only sounded when the 300-plus children in the lunchroom were collectively too loud. I took my walk of shame across the cafeteria with every child silently looking at me. I was one to get in trouble at home, but never at school. Even as I write, I feel hot just thinking about this awful moment. I waited in his office, so afraid that I wet my pants. Further shame. When he came in, I threw my arms around his legs and wept and begged for forgiveness. He sat me down, took his seat behind his big desk of authority and proceeded to tell me he had a mental list of the best students in the school and that I was no longer one of them. Once again, I was "bad." No matter how hard I tried, I was a grave disappointment.

That afternoon as I got on the bus to go home, my brother was already waiting for me with his arm outstretched — an invitation to his love and compassion. I folded into him and cried. How desperately I needed to feel loved. I looked out the window and saw the assistant principal looking at me. I had always liked her. She was pretty with blonde hair, blue eyes and a kind smile. This day, however, her smile had turned to a scowl. Once she knew she had my attention, she struck one pointer finger repeatedly over the other. It was that universal gesture chiding "shame on you." Any comfort from my brother's tenderness and compassion disappeared. Yes, I was a bad girl.

Voice of the Shadows

I entered high school with my gaping wound oozing and with a desperate for love. Nervous and awkward, I walked into a class filled with upperclassmen and was immediately investigated by the penetrating eye of a 19-year-old who also lived in the shadows, his much darker than mine. His ripped jeans and rugged plaid shirt matched perfectly with the guitar strapped to his chest and cigarette breath. How could this 19-year-old senior possibly like me? Didn't he know I was rejected by the 14-year-old boys my age? But he liked me a lot and that had never happened to me before. Though he was bad news, and I knew it, his attention and pursuit were poured out on a desert soul, and this led to three years of drinking deeply in the shadows with him.

He was abused as a child and never really loved by anyone. The evil and wretchedness he battled were brutal, and none of it had been resolved when he met me. This was my greatest challenge yet, to love and heal this man, and to rescue us both in the process. His attention and pursuit did its work, seemingly filling all of my emotional holes and I felt a love greater than ever before. Of course, it wasn't love at all but an intense and scorching flame that morphed and charred me from the inside out.

After several years and professional help, I found the courage to escape his shadows, a shell of my former self. His abuse dug deeper into my childhood wounds. But perhaps even worse than being sexually defiled was the verbal barrage of personal, physical insults that turned me against food and into a new love of self-hatred. Thinness at all costs became my new survival strategy. I was a tormented, skinny girl, literally hiding in the shadows. I disappeared into an empty room during lunch and took the long way to classes to avoid crowded hallways. I feared everyone and my reflection in the mirror was the worst enemy of all. I barely ate and took 14 laxatives a day to make sure anything I did eat left my body as quickly as possible. I lost 40 pounds in a matter of months, but somehow the thinner I got the more I hated myself and the louder the lies became. I would stand in front of the mirror naked, chanting over and over, "I hate myself, I hate myself. You are ugly, you are ugly." It's hard to explain, but these were the words I knew I needed to hear to encourage further punishment of myself. "Exercise harder, swallow more pills, eat less," were the words I repeated daily. The kidnapper was louder than ever. Now I was twice abused, and there was no getting away from who I really was. *"You are worse than bad. You are irreparable. You are defiled and damaged. You belong in the shadows. You will never be invited into the sun's rays of joy and freedom again."*

Oh, to be back in the woods with mama, dancing along the path and seeing the delight in her eye. There was no longer any part of me that was lovely. Even mama's eyes had grown weary. I was now a problem for her too. I knew she was aching for me. I knew she loved me deeply, but there was no mistaking that I was a cause for deep pain, great concern and was a source of exhaustion to everyone in my life. I longed to graduate, to get away from the proclaimed "Friendly City" of our town and go to someplace new where I could change my name, my colours, my course and hope for something new.

My Voice

College was a turn of the page, a brand new chapter. I followed my big sister Kristen (nearly six years older) to the University of Kentucky, where she had graduated, and then got married and made the bluegrass state her home. I felt safe knowing she was near. I dropped the "i" in Katie and officially became Kate. I packed up my hippie, thrift-store digs and made a trip to the mall, where the full-length mirror, as well as my mom and sister, agreed that this new image would set me well on my way to a fresh new start and a hopeful future. I resolved to find goodness and got involved in a Christian ministry, which was filled with kind and bright people. I quickly immersed myself in a group of girls, who all danced in the sun, and I felt like I belonged for the first time in a long while. It was here that I regained my appetite for food, life and people, and began to feed on delicious messages of the love of God and ideas of grace, forgiveness and new beginnings.

I grew up in the church. I had always believed in God and desperately wanted to "feel" His proclaimed love. There were two roadblocks that stood in my way: First, the thought that I was incapable of being loved by God. Second, that God wasn't as good as I had heard because, "Why would a good God create someone like me? Why would he have allowed the unfortunate events in my life if he loved me?" But now, being so immersed in a positive Christian culture and being so separate from the ghosts of my past, I was able to believe it, at least in part, because I so desperately wanted to be "one of those people." Unfortunately, these truths landed on top of 20 some years of bad memories and sneering lies. My heart became a boxing ring. Loved versus unlovable. Good versus bad. The lies nearly always won.

In my sophomore year of college, Kristen had her first baby, and I fell totally in love. Sweet baby Rebekah opened up a whole new room in my heart, and I began to know myself as a nurturer for the first time. When she was colicky, I would sing, she would grow quiet and I discovered that there was power in my voice. Like mama, I sang and spoke words over her that were true, and she gravitated toward me. She felt my love, and I felt hers. We had a special bond. This relationship was like ointment on a very old wound. My life began to have meaning, and my arms and heart would ache in between visits with her. The birth of Bekah brought something else into my life too: the return of haunting memories from my childhood. The kidnapper was unrelenting in his accusation that I would somehow hurt my niece and that I could not be trusted. I wrestled with this for weeks until I dared to talk to Kristen about it. I held Bekah one afternoon and waited until Kristen took a shower so I could talk to her without looking her in the eyes. The shame was too much to bear when she was looking at me.

"I won't hurt her, Kristen. I'll never hurt her," I sobbed. Kristen pulled back the curtain and just looked at me, so full of confusion and compassion, and at once got out of the shower. She got dressed, we sat on the front porch and through tears I told her everything about the dark experiences from my childhood. Kristen held me tight, and with her voice of truth she flushed out my wound over and over again. I was no longer hiding. I began to feel known and I felt compassion and understanding from one of the most important people in my life. Kristen was now a friend as well as my big sister, and being loved by her was the medicine I needed for my diseased heart.

Chris's Voice

A couple of years later, Chris came along. My knight in shining armour. He was different than the other guys I'd dated. He was so calm; so steady and laid-back. He was funny and had no agenda. He was tender and gracious with the stories of my past, and in each other we found refuge. I shyly opened my deceived ways of thinking to Chris, and his voice of truth was like water poured into my thirsty heart. He gave me something I so desperately needed. We were married 18 months later. I wore a white dress and for a moment I felt pure. I felt pretty. I was ready to put it all behind me and to walk into the fairy tale I'd always dreamed of. Our honeymoon quickly reminded me that sexual intimacy, though good and right with my new husband, was still loaded with shame and fear for me. Just when I thought I had escaped the kidnapper, he was there, his voice of accusation telling me that I was still bad. Neither love nor being chosen could change my true identity.

The first three years were a back and forth in love and pain. I had issues, Chris had issues, and we often had no idea how to love well or live well. But then we got pregnant, and I was filled with something pure, something lovely and for the first time in all my life, I felt permission to walk back into the sun. To twirl and dance with the rest of the glowing women who were chosen to be life-carriers. It was my turn to fully embrace the nurturing role I discovered when I became an aunt. Maybe I wasn't so bad after all? I was growing life — a beautiful, feminine little life named Anna, and I would protect her and love her forever. This was my truth. I would get the chance to duplicate the most precious relationship of my life: my own relationship with my mom. What a gift. Could this really be happening to me? She was our love project, and together we stood in the sun, until the eclipse came and blocked out all light and joy.

Anna's Voice

One day, I was sitting on the couch folding the last load of Anna's clothes. I smiled, folding every teeny tiny piece of pink until I realized it had been some time since I felt her move. Chris came home at 10:00 p.m. that evening from a basketball game and rushed me to the hospital after all of my tactics to coax her awake were unsuccessful. One nurse after another couldn't find her heartbeat. They told me that sometimes the baby would lay in such a way that they couldn't hear it. I believed them. Chris did not. He looked at me, held my hand and said, "Kate, no matter what happens, we are going to be okay." What was he saying? How could he possibly allude to such horror? I got angry.

"Don't say that," I snapped. He already knew his baby girl was dead.

The doctor walked slowly into our room with a somber, inquisitive look, carrying what I refused to believe. When he put the ultrasound probe on my bulging stomach, I stared at a motionless heart and screamed. My baby girl was gone. She was dead. I wailed and yelled the name of Jesus over and over. My only hope now could come from him. The doctor, who was also a Christian, with a rush of faith or maybe just compassion said, "Let me look again." Once again the monitor revealed that my precious, longed for Anna was gone. God was silent. He was immovable, even at the sound of my grief-filled wailing and pleading.

Three days later we delivered our Anna Rose Katherine. She was five-and-a-half pounds of pure beauty with a head full of thick dark hair and the sweetest, most kissable little mouth. She defined loveliness. I fell so much more in love with Chris that day. His smile was like a river wide. Even though his girl was gone, seeing her and touching her gave him so much joy. It was supernatural to behold. We had to compress a lifetime of love into a single day. Family and friends filled our room to say hello and goodbye to our little one. We watched our parents grieving for both their children and their granddaughter. After 11 hours of holding her, kissing her and singing to her, we cradled our girl for the last time as our kind nurse Alice took pictures. It was the most excruciating moment of my life, feeling the depth of my own pain, and bearing witness to the pain of my husband. We laid together in the hospital bed and wept with our girl in between us. Finally, I gave my daughter to Chris and watched as he placed her in Alice's arms. Alice then took a small stuffed pink hippo a friend had given Anna and placed it in my hands. "So your arms will not be empty," she said. I squeezed that little plush bundle tight and held onto Chris heaving as Alice walked out of the room with our daughter. It was everything I could do to keep from jumping up and running down the hall. I wanted to scream, "She's mine! She's mine, damn it. Give her back!" How could I have really just let someone walk away with my baby? But death had claimed her and I had to let her go. Chris and I gripped each other tightly, our hearts flooded with an unimaginable sorrow. Our long-anticipated daughter was gone. I still shudder at this moment in my life 13 years ago. This moment changed everything.

That was 2005, the year my baby died, and my heart shattered. I was among the living dead. I was utterly lost and undefined. I curled up into a cocoon of grief. It was the safest place to be and yet the scariest, most tragic season of my life. I had no idea it would also be the place where I would find healing and receive the gift of being redefined and repurposed in this world.

Speaking Truth

Over the course of three years, I worked with two counsellors who walked with me not only into the pain of the loss of my daughter but also the pain of all the years before. It was really a process of coming to see how the kidnapper had used every painful moment in my life to cement deception into the walls of my heart and mind. A lifetime of lies escalating to the death of my daughter led me to a screeching halt in my already fragile relationship with God. It was always hard for me to believe that He was good and even harder for me to believe that He could love "bad Katie." But this had done it; this had broken my heart wide open, and the kidnapper held me hostage as I raged against God. "You did this to me. You could've saved her, and you didn't. You are a liar. You are *not* good. You are *not* love," I would say. At the same time, I raged against myself. I would say things like, "This is all my fault. My body failed my girl. I must've done something wrong. He took her from me because He was protecting her. I wouldn't have been a good mother. God knew this, and He took her away. He was punishing me for a lifetime of failure."

But here is the unexpected thing that happened. As I sat with my counsellors with a bleeding and angry heart laid bare, they invited me to present that mess of a heart to God. *Could I really be that transparent? Would I not be struck instantly?* But with their confidence and the fact that I felt I had nothing else to lose, I spoke my lies, fears and hatred aloud. Quite astonishingly, I heard His voice, and it was nothing like the voice I feared. Through visions, I saw His face and eyes that both smiled and wept for me. This face was also not at all what I had feared. And yet, both His voice and His kindness felt so familiar. This was my first real experience that showed me the Jesus I'd heard about since I was a child, who was in fact full of compassion and love. Wasn't this what I'd yearned for all along? To have compassion and love? Could the death of my daughter —

something so horrid — actually be paving a path for me to finally know and experience the love of God?

For years, I had been hiding under my pain, trying to be a "good Christian." I was trying to be happy. Trying to do good. Trying to ignore the whispers of doubt, anger and blame. Trying to heap sweetness on top of the messy underbelly of disgust and shame. Trying to earn my place back in the sunlight. When I finally stopped trying to be and simple was, the real me was able to encounter the real Jesus, not the warped God the kidnapper had lied to me about. I was encountering the true God, the one who is risen and full of the kind of love I always dreamed about but figured could not possibly exist for a girl like me. The Jesus of the Bible became the Jesus of my grief. I discovered that the Good News I'd heard of since I was a little girl, was not just a story to be read, but a story I could live. This was the best news possible for a corpse of a grieving mother like me. One by one I came to him with my memories, my questions and my pain. He opened my eyes and my heart to His words of truth and His voice of love for me. I then came to understand the reason His tone and tenderness had been so familiar. My dear mother. It was her voice of acceptance, of understanding, of pride and unashamed love. Then an even greater revelation occurred. It wasn't that Jesus was like her, but rather, she was like Him. It was His love and His truth within her that spoke. Then I remembered my sister, my brother, my husband and all of the other voices of truth in my life. They were all speaking the language of the greatest love of all. "The voice" had always been His.

God's Voice

One of the sweetest gifts that came as a result of Anna's death, ("gifts of grief" I began to call them) was a restored relationship with my dad. Witnessing his heartbreak for Anna and me seeped deep into the roots of my childhood. The great wall the enemy had built between us that awful day 20 years ago was now crumbling. His tears fed my soul with the compassion, love and tenderness I'd always longed to receive from him. His heart was broken for me, "his baby girl." The Lord was pouring water from heaven on this wildfire of my heart and using my dad to soothe old and new flames. He became a confidant and a voice of truth and wisdom as I wrestled with questions like, "Who is God" and "Was this my fault?" My daddy's voice in this season was a true and kind voice that was reflective of the tone and tenderness of God. Though I had lost so much and grief was consuming me as a mother, I was simultaneously receiving life in the graveyard of my childhood. God was pursuing and restoring my heart much like He did with His chosen people recorded in the book of Hosea: "Therefore I will allure her into the wilderness and I will speak tenderly to her. I will make the Valley of Achor (of trouble) a doorway of hope. And there she will respond as in the days of her youth, as in the days she first came out of captivity." Hosea 2:14-16.

I had been captive my whole life, and though it cost me my daughter, this valley of trouble opened a doorway of Hope. My Anna was dead, but I was coming to life.

Spring had finally come. After a lifetime of being harassed by the kidnapper, the voice of truth finally had a face: Jesus, my rescuer. This didn't take away my pain. It didn't erase my losses but gave me comfort, peace, hope and a whole new and true identity. The winter cocooning season of disbelief and deepest sorrow was over, and I could finally emerge and spread my new wings — the ones that were always blueprinted inside.

Since the death of my daughter, I've come to realize that the path from pain to peace is not a journey travelled just once. Pain is a continual journey, with some days being harder than others. It's often life's sweetest joys that reacquaint me with the depth of my ache for Anna. For example, four precious sons came from my womb in the decade after losing my girl. Oh, the bliss they have each brought to us. First John, then Ben, then Elijah and Jonah. Four beautiful, sandy-haired, blue-eyed boys, all uniquely different and each wonderful.

Anna is irreplaceable, but parenthood could be restored. Our boys gave us that. To watch Chris coo, kiss and pray over his babies, and for me to rock, nurse and sing to my children has been magnificently healing. It's all such a wonder, an unspeakable delight, the joy of watching my sons live. And yet, that joy is always standing beside the immense sorrow because my daughter is gone. So yes, there is joy, but also there is pain. This is why it is so crucial that I listen to the voice of the rescuer and not the voice of the deceiver. These forces of good and evil are always talking to me. One seeking to steal my heart from truth and subsequent peace; the other seeking to woo me into the riches of truth and peace. Whom I choose to listen to dictates my quality of life.

I have also learned that life doesn't have just one big pitfall. Suffering one enormous tragedy in life doesn't excuse you from future tragedies. In the years since Anna's death, there has been immense sorrow. My college roommate adopted a precious baby boy who was diagnosed with leukaemia three months after she brought him home from Africa. He died 11 months later. Watching Raegan grieve for her baby was an excruciating pain that reopened my own wound. That same year, my husband's youngest brother suddenly and unexpectedly died at the age of 23. There are no words to describe the agony of watching my husband and his two other brothers lower their baby brother into the ground. There are no words to describe the hideous pain of watching my in-laws mourn their baby. It is an unspeakable sorrow, and yet, the rescuer's voice could be heard loud and clear. His presence of comfort and love was steadfast.

When I suffered two miscarriages last year, I grieved deeply. I ached for the loss of these little ones. These were babies that I'd hoped were the daughters I'd prayed for, for 12 long years. They were babies I had dreamed of and named, and babies I believed were promised to me by the good hand of the God I loved and trusted. Still, in all of this, the voice of the Shepherd could be heard:

"You will see the goodness of the Lord in the land of the Living." Psalm 27:13

Then my precious lifelong friend Kristin was diagnosed with cancer. The disease ravaged her and took her from her four precious babies and her beloved just one year after the diagnosis. I wept and lamented with heart-wrenching grief. But His voice was there.

My dear Krissy spent the last week of her life in a beautiful hospice house. I followed the ambulance in my car that took her from the hospital to her "final home." I walked into her room shortly after she arrived and watched as several nurses helped her to the bed. Upon seeing me, she smiled brightly and said to the staff, "My sister is here. This is my sister."

"It's so nice to meet Kristin's sister," the nurse responded. I corrected her and in a way apologized for the error.

"Actually, we are dear, lifelong friends," I said.

"We are sisters," Kristin softly and sorrowfully chided me. My heart sank as I was the one in error.

"Yes Krissy, we are *sisters*," I agreed. Oh, how I wish I could redo that moment.

My final goodbye with my "sister" was among the most sacred moments of my life. I climbed into her bed and curled my body around her small, fragile frame. She was no longer able to walk or eat or talk. She just was. There were moments of "coming to" and soft short words spoken, but life as my dear one had known it was gone. Courtney and Laurie, precious college friends were there too. Courtney sat at her feet, and Laurie sat at her side. We encircled our beloved friend and filled that room with immeasurable love and pain. I became overcome with the sense that I should speak to her. I whispered in her right ear everything I could think to say. I told her all about her loves, her sweet babies and her husband, and how they were doing. I told her how God was already meeting their deep needs. I told her about the funeral arrangements being made and the beautiful flowers that were being delivered, her very favourite in blush pinks and shades of white. I told her all about how God loved her and about how it was time for her to stop believing the lie that she wasn't "enough" and that she had not done "dying" well. I told her that very soon she would begin to see His face and His immense delight, a delight she struggled to believe in her sickness. And then we sang several of our favourite hymns, such as "Amazing Grace" and "Softly and Tenderly Jesus is calling." When I could think of nothing else to say, I grew quiet. At once, Courtney noticed Kristin's brow furrow.

We each ached for this pain and then she reached up and tugged at her ear and whispered a single word. Courtney understood her and said, "Kate, she said, 'Voice.' Keep talking to her." I began to speak again, softly in her ear. She breathed deep, her brow lines disappeared, and there was peace.

That night I went back to Kristin's house to stay with her children. I crawled into bed with each of her girls and tearfully obliged as they sadly requested, "Miss Katie, sing to me." I sang the same words I'd just sang to their mommy and spoke words to each of them about how very loved they were. They fell asleep peacefully in the midst of great darkness.

Later that night, after all four children were asleep, I laid on the couch and heaved deep sobs. I would never laugh or cry or be with my dear Krissy again. Her final whisper, "Voice" kept turning over again and again in my head. Then this scripture came to mind:

"My sheep hear my voice, and I know them, and they follow me. I give them eternal life, and they will never perish, and no one will snatch them out of my hand. My Father, who has given them to me, is greater than all, and no one is able to snatch them out of the Father's hand. I and the Father are one." John 10:27-29

I believe what we are all really yearning for, from cradle to grave, is the right voice to listen to. Whether we are wrestling with the pain of abuse, the loss of a child, the incriminating words of guilt and shame, having a hard time falling asleep or dying . . . we are all just crying out for *the* voice. There is a passage from the Bible I cling to these days:

> "If you abide in my word, you are truly my disciples. Then you shall know the truth, and the truth shall make you free." John 8:31-32.

His word is His voice. His voice is the truth. Truth will always bring freedom. The rescuer brings freedom. Isn't freedom what we are all searching for? Isn't that why my mother's voice had been so crucial in my life? It was the key to release me from my bondage, out of the deception that kept me locked in guilt, shame and self-hatred. And wasn't it the rescuer's voice that had delivered and continued to deliver me year after year in my grief? It was a voice, promising freedom from hopelessness. It was a presence bringing strength, comfort, provision and freedom from permanent suffering.

Two weeks after Kristin died, I had my first dream of her. She appeared across the room from me smiling. I ran to her and urgently begged, "Kristin tell me what to do for you. I'll do anything." She extended her hands and gave me a long strand of Christmas lights. "Hang up the lights," she said, with a curious, joyful grin. I woke the next morning so delighted to have seen my dear one smile. What a contrast to the grimacing of her last days. But Christmas lights in the middle of March? Why didn't she reiterate her caring for the children as she had before she died? Why in the world would she urge me to hang up Christmas lights? A month later we learned we were expecting and our due date was none other than Christmas Eve. Yes, I would hang up the lights for Krissy. I would plan for and anticipate the joy of our Christmas baby.

Our precious *daughter* came early, December 7th, a few hours before the day Kristin would've turned 41. We named our long-anticipated and prayed for daughter, Vivian Joy Noelle, after my precious Kristin Noelle.

How can I put into words the goodness of God for all of this? The dream of Kristin, and a Christmas miracle of a baby girl, after 12 years of praying and the loss of three little ones. How can I describe the joy of being able to love and care for a daughter, the closest earthly restoration for my loss of Anna? Not a replacement by any means, but the closest redemptive gift to the loss of our first daughter was the birth of our second. They are my bookend babies.

As I write these words, my precious Vivi is two months old. Already she responds to my voice. If she hears me, she turns, coos, smiles and cries for milk. She is already yearning for the sound of me. I will be a voice of truth for my darling girl. I will tell her who she is and who she is not. I will be a strong voice, and I will do everything within my power to protect her from the deceiver. He will certainly come close. He will try to snatch her heart from the place of truth. But I am aware of that tactic, and I will be louder and stronger and mightier than him. I will introduce my sweet girl to the rescuer, and she will understand that my voice is just a hint of the wonder and power of His. I pray she follows this voice. I pray she makes her heart His home and that her life is one experience after another in the freedom that comes from truth. A freedom that exists even in the midst of life's hurts and pains.

Freedom

Two days ago was my daughter Anna's thirteenth birthday. I dressed our boys, 12, 10, seven and four in jeans and button-up shirts. "Handsome like daddy," the youngest said. I placed Vivian, who was in a hot pink dress and bow, in their arms. I couldn't even muster a tear as Chris snapped a picture of this long-awaited moment. There was simply too much joy. But later that day, after the clothes had come off and celebrations had ended, I climbed into bed, retrieved my pictures of Anna and the small box of ashes I've never had the courage to open, and I laid in my bed and wept for the one that has permanently severed my heart. So much life and joy all around me and yet . . . I grieve her still. It was a moment that always feels very close to despair. A moment when the pain of her absence seems to swallow up everything. But then He was there:

"And I heard a loud *voice* from the throne saying, 'Behold, the dwelling place of God is with man. He will dwell with them, and they will be his people, and God himself will be with them as their God. 4 He will wipe away every tear from their eyes, and death shall be no more, neither shall there be mourning, nor crying, nor pain anymore, for the former things have passed away.'" Revelation 21:3-4

Through this, *His voice*, I was free from the bondage of despair. Once again, His voice spoke the truth, and at *His voice*, my pained heart was lulled back to peace. His words invited me to understand the hope that I have as a child of God. My Father is a force of love and compassion. A God who Himself aches at my grieving. A God who has a plan to wipe away my tears and to comfort me for all eternity. A God who I believe is even more eager than I for the reunion I will have with my heavenly girl and my dearest friend. My crying ceased. I placed Anna's pictures, and ashes back in their home in the velvet lined box on my dresser, and I emerged once again with wings outstretched, ready to fly into yet another season of freedom — the experience of hearing and believing His voice.

Voice of Truth

Have you ever felt like you were nearing an end, a resolution, and then you discovered there were many more miles to travel? This has very much been my experience as I have written these hard, deep and meaningful pages. I began this writing process much like an eager reporter, ready to detail my life as a memoir. Yet this writing process has revealed to me that I am still very much on a journey . . . still very attuned to the voice of shame and often handicapped by my own false beliefs and crippled ways of moving and relating in this world. At nearly 40 years of age, a life perhaps half lived, there are many chapters behind me; yet, many chapters of healing are yet to be written. Here is what I know and can offer confidently today regarding "The Voice of Truth."

Every day I can wake up and choose which song I will live by and dance to. I can listen to the voice that calls me by name, the voice that says I am created purposefully with a unique place and way to shine the light I've been given. Or, I can listen to the voice that hisses and sneers from the shadows and tells me I am worthless. The voice that says I am nothing, that reminds me of my past and recent failures, and insists that I will never be enough. The choice, daily, is mine to make.

Shame is not once conquered and never again confronted. Shame is a flaming error of the evil one that will come again and again. Shame is hidden within memories and conjured by long ago smells and a voice heard and absorbed can be a voice repeated. I can hear it as I size up into postpartum jeans, as I stare at saggy skin and fingernails still chewed on. I can hear it as I parent my children and speak and look with disappointment at those I love the most. I hear it when guilt escalates like a towering wave and regret bites like a shark. I can hear it as I write and fear what others will think of me, the woman who____. I could fill in many blanks. Overcoming shame requires an intentional stance against the wrong voice and to daily sprint toward the right one.

I have learned and am learning that anytime I sense negative emotions (shame, guilt, fear, anger, anxiety) that there is digging to do. These emotions are flags in the soil of my heart, signaling that there is something that needs to be unearthed, uprooted, and, in its vacancy, something new and beautiful to be planted. Something true, which will grow and produce the fruit of love, joy and peace for my own good pleasure and also for others to enjoy through me. For example, in my life, recent anxiety sent my digging into a hard space in my heart that unearthed an overwhelming and dominating belief that it is my job to make sure certain others are loved, perfectly, all the time. This belief was uncovered after weeks of chest pain and shortness of breath that led to blood work and a CT scan for what was initially thought to be a pulmonary embolism. After everything scary was ruled out, we realized my plummet was the result of terrific exhaustion, depletion and stress. As I dug deeper, an even greater lie was uncovered — that my worth and value is dependent on who I am rescuing. I was left blankly asking myself, "Who am I if I . . . stop?" In digging up these lies, there was and is space for truth. This is what "The Voice" has been saying to me most recently:

"Before you ever did, you were. Before you ever loved, you *were* loved. Before you ever blessed another, you blessed me. You are mine. You are enough. You were aglow with my light and love even as I was creating you in your mother's womb. The light was not turned on once you took centerstage and began impressing others. You have value and worth simply for who I created you to be and your value is infinite based on the fact that I without question died to rescue you from yourself, from your sin and from the deceiver. I am desperate to be yours and for you to be Mine. The thought of separation from you was too much for me to bear and so I sacrificed everything so I could hold you, have you, know you, love you, live within you and be yours forever. You have always been worth everything to me. No sacrifice would be too great to rescue you. And that is my name — Rescuer. It belongs to me and me alone. Please give it back. Please don't assume that role again. The weight and power of this name is reserved for me alone . . . it is too much for you to carry and always will be. Let me be God. Let me save. Let my love and sacrifice define who you are. Let grace win — not obligation or need. Be still Kate and know that I am God." Psalm 46:10

I love these newly planted words of His — the gardener of my heart. I find myself on tired anxious mornings, sitting in this newly tilled soil, running my fingers through the soft green tendrils of life, smelling their fragrance, drinking in their loveliness, and finding power and peace to begin another day in the truth.

Another important lesson I am learning in this season of my life is the need for, and power of, forgiveness. As I unearthed deception, I was confronted with the pain, bitterness and resentment that I was carrying toward others, including myself. Forgiveness at its root is about what you did not get that you wanted. I am learning that to forgive does not condone the offence or excuse the pain. Forgiveness is a liberating act of grace that empowers one to live separately from the belief that someone must continually pay for the wrong done or the unmet want or need you carry. Forgiveness allows you to see all mankind as equally and desperately in need of the grace and forgiveness of God, and to harness that grace for ourselves. Then we can in turn extend that same grace to others. Forgiveness is freedom. The deceiver will convince you of the opposite. He will lead you to think that forgiveness is weakness and that power and safety comes in the way of bitterness and unforgiveness. For many years I listened to this voice and wept in my own bondage. It is a liberating experience to forgive and to feel compassion in the place once black with blame. By inviting forgiveness into my life, I have also welcomed in greater love, peace and joy into places once shackled with resentment.

My first book is called *The Jesus of My Grief: From Pain to Peace Through Visions of the Savior.* Perhaps this chapter should be named The Jesus of my Shame: From Bondage to Freedom Through the Voice of the Rescuer. Either way one thing is clear: He is My way, My truth and My life, and I have come home to the perfect love of the Father through Him! John 14:6

In my dear Krissy's dying weeks and moments, I sang the following words of a beloved hymn again and again to her and to her babies. I sing them now to myself and to my Vivi as I rock her to sleep. In my living and in my eventual dying these words are my compass. They guide me to the One whose voice is altogether trustworthy and true and in them I find life and peace. I offer them now to you, my friend, as the most precious gift I possess:

Softly and tenderly Jesus is calling
Calling for you and for me;
See, on the portals He's waiting and watching,
Watching for you and for me.
Come home, come home,
You who are weary, come home;
Softly and tenderly Jesus is calling . . . calling for you and for me.

[Song writer: Will Thompson]

CHAPTER 3

Sometimes Coffee, Sometimes Tea

I AM Contessa T. Thomas

A sharp pain ripped through my back as I laid sleeping in the early hours of that Friday morning. "Is this finally it?" I thought. "Will I finally be released from this agony?" I had been in labour for 14 days straight. I stayed perfectly still and waited. As I began to relax, another surge of pain slowly moved through my lower back. I wished for the sun to rise and bring with it my release from the pain. I longed for my husband's return from New York and wondered if he would make it back in time for the birth of our third child.

We had relocated to Maryland 11 months earlier, but my husband's job was still in New York — a four-hour drive away from our current residence. Ethan stayed there for the entire week and came home on the weekends. So, I was all alone in this painful experience. I longed to see the comforting faces of my neighbours who were most certainly asleep in their apartment downstairs.

How will I get to the hospital? I don't want to have to wake up my neighbours. Who is going to take care of my children until my husband returns from work?

These questions held my mind captive, as though I was on an endless merry-go-round. In a slight state of panic, I called my sister, Candace. As she sleepily answered the phone, I blurted out with great urgency, "I think I am in labour now."

"Tessy, are you sure?" she asked.

"Yes, the contractions are coming strong and very close together," I replied.

As her voice intensified, she asked me, "So what are you going to do? Did you call Ethan?"

"No, I didn't call him yet because I do not want to wake him up," I said.

"Call him now and then call your neighbours downstairs" my sister commanded. She knew my backup plan was to have my neighbour take me to the hospital if Ethan was not able to get back in time.

I immediately hung up the phone and called my neighbour downstairs, who picked up rather quickly.

"Janelle, I am so sorry to wake you. I apologize, but I'm in labour," I told her.

She responded without hesitation, "I am coming upstairs right now to help you get dressed, and my husband will take you to the hospital." Then she hung up the phone.

Within two minutes, Janelle was there comforting me and helping me to put my clothes on. This moment reminded me of how we met. Only a week into living in our new apartment, my daughter — who is a little ball of energy — was jumping and flipping in our bedroom. My neighbour's husband worked nights and slept in the day. Out of frustration, he took a broomstick and started to hit the ceiling to let us know to stop the noise. Wanting to be on good terms with her new neighbours, Janelle came running upstairs and knocked on my door to apologize.

From that day on, our families became inseparable; our children constantly played together. I would give advice to her eldest son and daughter, and shower them with that 'motherly' kind of love — one that was sincere and non-judgmental. On busy evenings, we would sometimes take turns hosting dinners at our apartments. Her dear husband also stepped right in and helped me out with household repairs that I was not able to do on my own during the week. Janelle and I would often escape to each other's apartments during the day when the children were at school, to confide in each other about our marriages, aspirations and fears. We shared tears of joy and sorrow, and really became a genuine source of support for one another. It still breaks my heart to remember her tear-stained face when I broke the news to her that we would be returning to New York after the birth of the baby.

Going along with the very nature of our friendship, she remained by the bathroom door as I groaned deeply in pain as the contractions kept coming. In fact, with every groan I knew that she wanted to burst through the bathroom door like superwoman to save me. Yes, my beautiful neighbour and her husband were my God-sent angels.

God truly knows our needs and supplies them way before we know that we will have need of them. My life is a living testimony of that. By that Friday afternoon, my husband and I welcomed the long-awaited arrival of our little boy, Elijah Axel Thomas. The birth of Elijah marked a pivotal point in my life. It was a time of great spiritual, mental and emotional growth — one that was well needed. It was the moment I fully embraced my life's journey and accepted my becoming.

The Struggle is REAL!

It seemed nothing in my life ever came easy. I would often observe the lives of others and silently ask the God of the Universe the question: "How come things never come easy for me?" Oppositions and struggles always seemed to impose themselves into my profession, education and relationships.

Professionally — being a woman of colour made my corporate progression challenging. I felt as if I had to jump twice as high as my Caucasian male peers to achieve only a fraction of their accomplishments.

"Sometimes coffee, sometimes tea."

Educationally — I had to pay my own way through school and struggle to maintain the crucial balance of work, life and school. There were times I would look at my privileged peers and pray to God to help me not resent them.

"Sometimes coffee, sometimes tea."

Relationships — I was so closed off to finding love. Dating for me was exhausting. I waited patiently for the guy to show me at least one fault, so that I was justified in dismissing him.

"Sometimes coffee, sometimes tea."

That soul defining saying, "Sometimes coffee, sometimes tea," is one of my wise grandmother's favourite sayings. My grandmother, Amanda Esterine, a.k.a. "Mama," has a wisdom that attests to the power of the Almighty Creator.

Every day either my sister Candace or I would call her to have morning devotion.

On one particular morning, after greeting each other and her asking about my well-being, I broke down and started telling her about the challenges that I was currently facing in my life as a wife and stay-at-home mother of three.

With a loving tone she said, "Tessy hush. I know what you are going through. I have been through some of the same things. Don't worry. Keep moving forward with God. Remember life is *"sometimes coffee, sometimes tea."*

Such a simple phrase, but what truth it bears. As many of us can attest, life is full of so many surprises. These moments of amazement, whether good or bad, start from the time that we take our very first breath, entering this world, and stretch all the way to our very last one. Guess what is the biggest thing about these moments? We usually do not have any control over them. We must learn to adjust in order to survive, and simply "roll with the punches." We have to quickly digest the fact that life is "sometimes coffee, sometimes tea."

After many years of revisiting that saying, I realized the purpose of my struggles. My life mimicked the refining process of a diamond. Initially, a diamond begins as a piece of coal embedded deep within the earth. After exposure to extremely high temperatures, pressures and eventually a volatile eruption, it shimmers with pure beauty. The hardships of my past and present moulded my character and refined my spirit into the beautiful person God wanted me to become. The struggles were designed to help me achieve my full beauty and potential from the inside out.

The Tortoise and The Hare

There is a saying, *"It is not about how you start, but rather how you finish."* There is certainly a lot of truth to it. Nonetheless, I do realize how you begin significantly impacts the tone of your life. Will it be calm and delightful, or painful and dark?

Life has definitely taken me on a wild-west adventure, and it still has me on its ride. Wednesday, June 5th, 1985 marked the beginning of the rollercoaster ride I refer to as "my life." That day was a rainy one, ladled with fog. If I could choose the ideal day to be born on, I would have chosen a bright and sunny one. However, that is life! Certain things are completely out of our control, but we must do our best to accept and move on to the next chapter that awaits us.

I was born at Queens General Hospital in Jamaica, Queens, New York (a public city hospital). According to my mother, my birth was an uneventful one for the most part. She was discharged within a few days after having me and I went home to start my new life with my father, mother, and big sister, Candace.

We lived in a one-bedroom basement apartment off Linden Boulevard in Queens. From my earliest recollection, it was a very small and dim place. Yes, I know it doesn't sound too appealing at all. However, that is all my mother and father could afford at the time — both of them were recent immigrants from the island of Jamaica.

Merlene Sylvia Esterine — I knew her as mommy, but who is she outside of that? That is a question that I desperately sought to answer for a large portion of my childhood and young adult years. She is a true woman of mystery. The factual stuff is easy to digest. For example, I accept with no reservations that she was born to Pasco and Amanda Esterine, on October 5th, 1958, in Jamaica. She took her formal place amongst their family as the seventh child and second daughter. However, the emotional and grey areas of my mother's personality always left me in need and feeling neglected.

Throughout the years there would be moments where my mom and I were alone and I would use the opportunity to get to know her better. This included learning about her origins and her childhood. I was not shocked to find out that she was very gentle in nature. The very trait that would make her the perfect candidate for her abusers.

My time spent in the apartment were fleeting. By the time my little brother came along about two years later, we had moved into a nice ranch-style house on the opposite side of town, off Linden Boulevard. As nice as that house was, it was marked with dark episodes of abuse.

My father loved to drink hard liquor (his drink of choice was rum), and when he got drunk (which was quite often), he would turn into an angry and abusive person. He would burst through the front door with the ever-present expletive "f**k you!" and would beat my mom for the silliest reasons when he was under the influence. This pattern would go on until I was about five years old. After he threatened to kill me while intoxicated, my mom decided that she was going to run away for good with my two siblings and I.

Have a Very Merry Christmas…NOT!

December 26th, the day after Christmas, started off like any other. Then my dad came thumping through the front door with his breath heavily saturated with alcohol, yelling, "I feel like killing somebody!" Candace and I stared at our mom with a puzzled look of concern. Even though we were just seven and five years old, we knew that something was not right with this situation.

"George, you are drunk," said my mom.

"F**k you, Sylvie. I feel like killing somebody," responded my dad.

I did not know that I was his target — his own child! My skin proved to be too light for his liking. It made him question if he truly was my father. I felt small, like an outcast. I remember asking myself, "Why am I a different skin tone from my siblings? Why did my father not want me because of the colour of my skin, which had nothing to do with my immense love for him?"

Everyone in the family was a darker skin tone, except for me. However, what my dear father never took into consideration was that genetics play a major role in an individual's appearance.

The liquor literally impaired his ability to be rational. It never occurred to him that even though my mom was a darker skin tone, she carried the lighter skin-tone genes (my grandmother and aunts had a fairer skin tone).

That was the straw that broke the camel's back. My mom was not going to sit back and let her husband kill her child. She ran for her life and the lives of her children. "Come kids, put on your shoes and coats now. We have to go!" said my mom.

We then left our house and went to the nearby Rib Shack restaurant, which was a little over two blocks away. We knocked on the door of a stranger and asked to use their phone to call 911. That was the beginning of the end of my parent's marriage.

The police met my mom at our house, where she grabbed all the belongings that she could, and we left to go and stay with her close friend. "Mommy I want to go back home to daddy!" my tiny voice shrieked.

I remember that day and the pain I felt, even at the tender age of five. I knew that life was going to be different for my siblings and me from now on, and I knew that it would also involve me seeing less of my dad. I cried my eyes out so badly that day; I wished with all my heart that the day's events would just disappear and that life would return to normal. Looking back at it now, I can see this was quite a contradiction. Nothing about my life was normal. It took me over 20 years to finally realize that.

Life kept moving right along as it usually does. We spent a brief time with my mother's friend and shortly after that we went to live with my aunt and her three children for a year. From that home, my mother moved out and began living with the man who would soon become my stepfather.

My first impression was that he seemed like a very nice man. I would even say he looked like he would be a good father. Little did we know that my mom was repeating a pattern. Her yearning for love and acceptance would extend an open invitation for the devil himself to walk into our lives. Just like my father before him, it was not long before he began physically abusing my mother.

The physical abuse was usually confined to my mom. However, one day during one of the attacks, my older sister Candace said to him, "You are going to go to jail for beating up my mom."

In that moment, time seemed to stand still as the entire atmosphere in the room grew darker as my stepfather took step by fervent step towards my older sister. I stood there with a horrified look on my face and felt absolutely helpless as he punched Candace.

I wanted to jump on his back and do something, anything to rescue her. But, my six-year-old body was frozen in the moment of shock and fear. As I stood there watching this horrifying scene unfold, I was crying and silently whispering, "No, please stop!"

What had come over my poor sister? Why would an eight-year-old say such a brave thing in a time of such imminent danger? She literally risked her young life at that time and paid dearly for it. She was simply speaking the truth in the moment, to stop our stepfather from hitting our mom. As I stood there and watched him create such havoc, my heart grew colder and it began to fill with more hate. I developed a feeling of not wanting to be loved, and it grew stronger. If this was love, I wanted no part of it.

Oh Love, Oh Love, Where Are You?!

In our home, the words "I love you" were never spoken. Instead, "I love you" was more of an action phrase.

"Kids dinner is ready!" … I love you.

"Kids, I am going to work now to provide for you!" … I love you.

"Kids, I will take a beating for you!" … I love you.

My mother loved with actions. My stepfather, on the other hand, had never learned a love language. He sat like a fat cat perched on a fence. He ate everything she offered and even the things she didn't. Everything emotional, physical, sexual and spiritual was taken by him. We were lucky if we got some of the leftovers.

My mom became very withdrawn as a coping mechanism and never said the words my sisters and brothers yearned to hear during our early years. We felt unloved from all corners of life. At one point in my life, I started to resent the woman that gave me life and wrote her off as weak. I was so angry! How could she let this man do this to us? How could she let him beat us so badly, when we were not even his children? WEAK! That was my answer to it all, and I became as cold as Elsa from the Disney movie Frozen. Anyone who crossed my path would definitely feel my wrath, and I didn't care — NO MERCY! Though I desired and yearned for love, my anger led me to disconnect from everyone and everything. It was the only way I knew how to survive.

As the years passed, the abuse from my stepfather grew worse. A year after the birth of my little sister (fourth child), my mom gave birth to another girl (fifth child). Three years later came the birth of my little brother, who would become my mom's last child — bringing her total number of children to six. Three children for my father, and three children for my stepfather. "Just great!" I thought, "Now I have to share my space with three other brats!" Even as I write these thoughts, they bring me pain, but I hated my life during that time. I really did. We were all spiralling down a slippery slope, and then a miracle happened. The "savage beast" was arrested and sent to jail for a crime he committed years before he met mother. My siblings and I were so happy that the monster was finally gone.

The Wolf in Sheep Clothing

"Children, Johnny is coming home," she broke the news to us so calmly. My heart stopped for what seemed like a few seconds. She then continued, "I also married him in jail, so that they would not deport him back to Jamaica."

I looked at her with a straight face and great pity in my heart. I wanted to go to my mom, shake her shoulders with great vigour and scream, "How could you have done such a thing? How could you be so stupid? He is a liar and has not changed!"

My intuition easily caught the scent of Johnny's lies — like a pile of freshly laid dog manure on the hot pavement of a New York City block. The smell was overwhelming, to the point where I wanted to vomit. I knew that he was deceiving my mom. He was using her and had a hidden agenda. "Why can't my mom see through the fabrication? Why? Why? Why?" I would ask myself. Sadly, the reality was that my mother was blinded by her love for this man.

Not too long after he stepped foot back into the house, the abuse returned — and this time it did with a vengeance. "God, please help us!" was all I could whisper each night as I tried to lull myself to sleep. At that time, I was around 12 years old and I suffered from high anxiety, which led to multiple panic attacks. The pressure of life was getting too much for me, and all I wanted to do was leave it. I was in a very DARK place. I thought about taking my life a few times, just so that I could escape this situation.

Delivered

Over time, my anxiety became so bad that an emergency room doctor was threatening to put me on anti-anxiety medication. I was going to have to go on medication if I didn't learn how to control it on my own, through deep breathing techniques and meditation. Something needed to happen quickly, and I believe that God knew that it was becoming more than my mother, siblings and I could bear — and He sent a remedy.

God's deliverance came in the form of my stepsister, who was my stepfather's first child (not with my mom). At first, it seemed like her presence was making everything more difficult. She was outspoken, rude and frankly did not care at all for the man she begrudgingly called "father." However, to our surprise, she was actually a blessing in disguise.

My stepsister was no easy cup of tea to sip. At first she did not like my mom because of the horrible stories her mother told her about my mother. After she moved in she saw that my mother was nothing like the picture painted by her mother. Almost instantly she started to like my mom and stood up for her when her dad became abusive. She also took a great liking to my siblings and me.

She would rebel in school and get into a lot trouble even though she knew a beating was inevitable. Her skin was often marked with black-and-blue bruises from the beatings inflicted by her father on her extremely fair skin. Little did we know, those highly visible bruises on her body would serve as the road map leading to our freedom.

One evening my stepsister came into the bedroom Candace and I shared and whispered to us, "Guess what?"

Candace and I hesitantly responded, "What?"

"I got suspended from school!" she said.

Candace and I both looked at each other in fear, and asked as if with one voice, "What did you do?" We knew all too well what was going to happen once her father found out.

Almost instantly, as if he sensed us talking about it, my

stepfather entered our room. The overall atmosphere in the room changed; it became dark as a great evil towered over our heads. Before Candace and I could blink, he was choking his daughter! As if choking wasn't terrible enough, he then proceeded to pick up the umbrella from Candace's bunk bed and press the release button, which caused it to forcefully hit her in the eye. We were horrified! Our poor mom could only look on in pure sadness and fear, because if she dared open her mouth she would be next.

The following day, my stepsister's eye was black and bruised — this marked the beginning of the end of my stepfather's dictatorship. She went to school that day as her suspension was not yet finalized. She told the counsellor how her dad beat and choked her the evening before. This led the school to report it to the city (Child Welfare Services) and a case was opened against him.

The seven of us were all taken away from my mom and were not returned to her until my stepfather vacated the home. That time seemed like the longest week of my entire life. Thankfully, he left our home, never to return.

It felt as if a big brick had been lifted off of my chest. Unfortunately, his departure was too late, as I had already dived into the deep end of the "unloved" pool and was drowning. My stepfather's leaving did not repair my heart as I thought it would. No, that true relief would come with me giving my life to God and being baptized at the age of 13.

Growing Pains

Yeshua (many know him as "Jesus") made all the difference in my life. The church was the only place where I truly felt free. At the church we met a group of individuals who took us under their wings, as if we were their own children. They showed Candace and I love and said the actual words "I love you."

Eventually, we were baptized and began our journey along the Christian pathway. I no longer felt like I was confined to a dark place of despair. I could finally see the light, as I was getting to know God for myself and growing in my faith with Him each day. I no longer thought about taking my life, but rather giving it to Him daily, so that He could direct my steps in helping others, including my mom and younger siblings.

I have vivid memories and know that prior to age 13, I was never happy. I had no sense of how it felt to be truly content before I surrendered my life to God. Life had me enclosed in its cocoon for what felt like an eternity, and now a different kind of transformation process was taking place — I was being awakened.

The years passed by quickly from that point on. Before I knew it, I was 21 and a college graduate. I was also married. I would have never imagined this would be me as a young woman. I was so closed off and didn't even like dating.

I was academically driven and had big plans for my life. My future plans included attending a prestigious law school and earning my law degree, becoming a successful lawyer, and buying a huge house for my mom and siblings. However, as the saying goes, "Man makes plans, and God laughs." I never expected that I would be married in my last year of college.

I experienced a complete life fusion (like a blood transfusion, but with one's life instead). My life turned out completely different from how I imagined it would be. For the most part it was a great thing. I learned how to love again, and that truly helped me to open my heart to another individual — in spite of my abusive past. I wish that I could end the story here with a happily ever after, but that is not how life usually works.

Remaining consistent with the underlying theme of my life — those moments of surprises still appeared, whether or not I was prepared for them. I gave birth to my first son, Christian, at the age of 23, and then about three years later I had my daughter, Joelle. My hands and heart were truly filled with joy.

Marriage in my opinion is a beautiful thing. However, it does come with great challenges and moments of highs and painful lows. My husband Ethan and I have been through some really trying situations during the course of our 11-year marriage. There were some awesome high points, and disappointing low ones as well. I wish that I could only focus on the happy times, and zip through the bad ones. However, that is not how life works.

Being a young married couple was quite challenging because we were still developing and becoming the people that we aspired to be — while also being responsible for each other and the lives of our children. What complicated matters even more was that I said "I do" to my husband during a time when I was fragile and didn't really know who I truly was. That became a reoccurring thorn in our marital life.

I wish someone would have stopped me and told me to first figure out my personal issues before merging my life with another individual. Unfortunately, no one did. To be 100 per cent transparent, I don't even think it would have made a difference. I made up my mind that I needed better. As a result, I adapted a one-track view. I had to learn the hard way — through my own experiences.

When we started dating, I wanted to escape my world of sadness and enter a much happier one with him. For the first time, I witnessed what a loving father should look like.

Ethan's family was the complete opposite of mine, and his father was that picture-perfect dad that we all wished we had. In fact, his father literally became "my dad." He taught me how to drive and how to be a great scholar.

He really opened my eyes to the fact that all men aren't bad. It was through my father-in-law that I learned that there were still good men in the world. This was the deciding factor in me marrying my husband. My heart was reassured knowing that he was raised by a man like his dad. It gave me hope.

It may sound like my life would have a fairytale book ending. Well, not so much. As the years went by in our marriage, I started to become very independent and I knew what I wanted in life. I love my husband dearly, but I do feel that this was not the Contessa that he signed up to spend the rest of his life with. So this created friction in our relationship, and at times pushed me backwards to a place where I had fought so hard to never enter again: the "dark" side.

I didn't feel the love and acceptance that he promised to give me. If my actions were not in line with what he deemed feasible, the silent disapproval process would start. Other times, I would feel as if his love was completely conditional; it was based on what I did for him. I honestly believe that I was sending out so many insecurity signals that his immediate response was to dominate and dismiss.

I was being starved of the very thing I had been yearning for my entire life. I had to earnestly pray and ask God to please keep me moving forward toward the light. There were plenty of times when I wanted to jump ship and get a divorce. However, I stayed put and prayed that God would see us through those turbulent episodes.

I was hopeful back then because I really wanted our marriage to be successful. The road has not been an easy one, and to this day it still keeps putting forth unexpected detours and roadblocks. Nonetheless, I am still trucking along on life's journey, with great faith in God.

The Year of Change

The year 2016 marked a major turning point in my life. It was a year of major changes indeed!

In this year I resigned from the only job I had since graduating from college (nearly 10 years of employment). I left everything and everyone that I knew and we packed up our family and moved to Maryland. There I became pregnant with my "miracle" rainbow baby boy, Elijah Axel, and formed SisArias United — an inspirational blogging business. It was also the year that would lead to my true moment of freedom — the moment I became more of the woman that I always aspired to be.

I was on the brink of breaking through the now transparent walls of the cocoon that I had been enclosed in since my early teenage years. I had blossomed into a strong Christian woman, who was getting ready to face the world and stand firm in the purpose that she was designed for by the

Creator. Leaving my job of nearly 10 years and taking a leap of faith was just another one of those situations where I had to stand strong — and stand strong I did.

SisArias United

SisArias is an inspirational blog website that my sister Candace and I first thought of when I relocated to Maryland, in July 2016. One day our regular phone discussion turned into how we could use our past life experiences to help encourage others to reach their full potential and overcome life's many hurdles.

During that conversation, we lightly touched on starting a blog website to do just that. The idea seemed very tangible. To sweeten the pot, we always dreamed and often talked about working together. God placed this burning desire in our hearts for years, and now we finally had a tool which we could use to spread our message to the world.

At the beginning of August 2016, we prayerfully brainstormed about a name for our business—and came up with SisArias United. The name stands for **Two Sisters** (Sis), **Two Stories** (Arias), **in One** (United). Our website officially launched September 2016, and the rest has been history.

Twice a week a blog article is released on our site (Sundays and Thursdays), that is both inspiring and educational.

Candace and I alternate when writing and posting our material. It has truly been a blessing for us both.

God has blessed me with Candace. She has been nothing but a support to me throughout the years — no matter how good or bad the times were. I cannot say that I have always been the best sister to her in return, but since I turned 18, I have been trying to put in overtime to make up for all the lost years. Candace was and still is an inspiration to me, and I love my sister with my entire heart. We still have great work to do, but I know together we are going to move mountains with God in the driver's seat of our lives.

To all the women out there who are struggling — don't give up! Hang in there and keep striving to be better. Prayerfully seek out the paths in life where God wants you to go. Remember, many times the journey will entail a lot of hills and valleys, but hold on. Through every hill and valley that you encounter, there is a lesson to be learned. Believe me when I say that the lesson, if used correctly, can convert negative energy into a powerful positive force that cannot be reckoned with. As well, these life lessons will help to strengthen your emotional, mental, spiritual and even physical muscles.

Just remember: life is "sometimes coffee, sometimes tea."

CHAPTER 4

Center Stage

I AM Ajua Phillips

I walk onto the stage and give the audience what they desire to see. They see a confident woman with her chin held high; a self-assured woman who has it all together. With boldness I walk to the podium and grab the microphone. I am home. I belong on this stage. I am ready to speak.

"Thank you for your kind introduction. Simply put, I am a wife, mother, daughter, sister, entrepreneur, volunteer, realtor, activist, and more importantly, God's unique creation," I say as the audience looks upon me and smiles. They have been waiting a long time to hear my voice.

"I have numerous letters beside my name, and I am in the process of acquiring more!" The crowd is pleased with my claim. "When is it enough? Is it ever enough? For me, the answer is an emphatic no!" My statement brings a roar of laughter from the crowd. What they cannot see is that despite being physically there in the moment, I do not remain with the crowd. As I always do, I fade away and hide behind my words. I drift to another world, even as I do the thing I was born to do.

Roles

I strut my stuff every day. I enter into a room and I capture people's attention with my style, my confidence and my façade. What lies behind this mask? Every time I open my mouth, I am performing. I know how to pull people in. I know how to make people feel special. Most of the time, I do it out of a genuine interest in the person. Other times, I have a motive — an ulterior one.

For example, in my life as a contractor, I always knew what to wear to tease people. I dressed in a way that had my attire on the brink of being inappropriate. It always left them wanting more; I almost always got what I wanted.

In my other life as a banker, I knew the right words to say, which appeared to promise my clients more without really promising anything or compromising myself.

In my life as a wife, I knew how to get my husband to do what I wanted. In the beginning, it was by expecting that I would always get what I wanted. Why wouldn't I expect to? When that stopped working, I resorted to tears. Then I moved to defiance, and then seduction. Now, I do something entirely different. I allow the most authentic part of myself to show up and remain present. It works!

As a mother, all I do is love my children. It does not always get them to do what I want, but a mother's love for a child is not conniving, and neither does it have strings. It just is. Aside from God's love, that is the greatest love of all. (I'm channeling my inner Whitney Houston here.)

My daily reality is that I strut. I light up on my stage. My stage is my daily life — as a wife, mother, aunt, sister, friend, daughter, realtor, motivational speaker and even as another driver on the road. Sometimes, I light up positively and other times negatively, as I want to take control of everything and everyone around me. But I ask myself sometimes, am I sucking up all the air in the room? Is it too much to want to take centerstage all the time? Do I allow others to be themselves? Is this light that I exude an all-positive one for myself and anyone who happens to fall under the rays?

The sad but obvious answer is:
Yes — I sometimes suck up all the air in the room.
Yes — I do want to take control.
Yes — I am sometimes overpowering and too much for some people to handle.
No — not everyone, myself included, always experiences my light as positive.

It is not entirely a bad thing to be confident and able to take charge. There are commendable aspects to it. There is a fine line between a confident, take-charge persona and a confident, "run over anyone in my way" persona. One has to know how to straddle it and come out on the positive side.

Centre Stage

For most of my childhood, I fancied myself as the next Diana Ross, complete with the long, flowing hair and stunning evening gowns. That was my delusional dream for a very long time. It was delusional because my voice was awful! I always wondered why I did not get compliments in church when I belted out hymns at the top of my voice. In retrospect, I think I even remember getting some odd stares from people; stares I interpreted as looks of admiration rather than bemusement. I was devastated when my husband told me that my vocal talents were frankly "sub-par." My lifelong dream of being on stage had been crushed, so why would I still feel alive whenever I was on stage? Could it be because it was a different stage?

Someone once told me that she watched me on a discussion panel and said to herself, "I want to be just like that woman!" It was very flattering. More importantly, it reaffirmed my belief that centre stage is where I belong. She went on to explain that I exuded a strength and presence that she admired and aspired to have one day.

What she did not know were the struggles I have gone through in my life. Regardless, I fed off the accolade.

One of my recently discovered strengths, is my ability to recognize what I am good at and make sure everyone else knows that I know I am good at it. I have not always owned my strengths. In fact, I downplayed them for a greater part of my life. I did not feel I was worthy of them or that anyone saw them as positive qualities. In some situations, I felt I had to hide my light so that others could shine. I have come full circle and a half. Now I own them and stop short of ramming them down people's throats. It's like I want people to pay for all the years I was bullied, taunted, sexually abused and ignored. Underneath this new self-confidence was a bitterness that only very few trained eyes could see. It was a paradox: I was confident yet insecure.

My husband asked me once, "Why are you so bitter?" I answered, "I am bitter because the world owes me something."

This internal struggle has affected more than just myself; it has affected my relationships. My daughter told me that I always want to control her. My son said that I always make things about me. My niece said that I do not really hear her. One of my oldest friends once said to me, "You always want to be the only one talking."

Centerstage. Centerstage. Centerstage.

There is nothing wrong with wanting to take centerstage. It is *how* you take centerstage that matters. My current perspective is that I can take centerstage and still allow others to shine. The fact that others shine does not diminish who I am. We can all shine simultaneously.

There are different stages in my life's journey. I transitioned from one to the next, hoping to get better with each consecutive stage. Now I have metamorphosed just like the butterfly. I started off as an innocent Egg in my mother's womb. Then, I hatched into a Caterpillar (Larva), where all I wanted to do was play and eat. This Caterpillar stage was a bitter-sweet idyllic childhood. I grew up fast. Faster than I should have. At that young age, I knew things that only grown women should. I shed my skin a number of times as a coping mechanism.

Then, my character was set — or so I thought. My exterior was hardened, so that I could protect myself. This Pupa/Cocoon stage allowed me to acknowledge, experience and deal with life in different ways. Then I emerged from my cocoon into the butterfly that I am today.

Mongoose

Let me take you back in time and tell you a story about a little girl who went into boarding school at the tender age of 10. She was very shy and sheltered. She cried every day when she saw the bridge she would cross with her parents on her way to her boarding school. She cried for three years, each year getting better but she still missed home. She made a number of friends, but she was still very insecure.

One day she sat innocently on her bed, not realizing her life was about to change forever. It was a normal day; nothing extraordinary. She woke up. She prayed. She made her bed. She showered and got ready for the day. She never imagined what was to come. She never imagined the violence that would bleed into her day and how much this experience would impact the rest of her life.

That day was supposed to be mundane like any other. She moved like a robot doing usual and predictable things. By mid-morning, she began to hear whispers and noticed that all was not right. By late afternoon, she heard a loud noise coming from somewhere; she did not understand what was going on. She heard muffled chants of a word she could not make out. The noise grew louder and louder until it became clear what they were chanting.

She ran out to see what all the commotion was about. Then she realized that it was about her. She heard her name, then the chant: "Mongoose! Mongoose! Mongoose!" She had never heard that word, much less knew the meaning. Suddenly, she found herself in the middle of this crowd of students chanting at her. She was confused, scared, helpless and crying all at once. She looked around for a friendly face. There was none.

Her "friends" all looked different. Not one friendly face among them. They looked like the monsters she had seen in all those horror movies she wasn't supposed to watch. Ghoulish. Freakish. Living and breathing poltergeists. She held her breath and tried to control the tears. She looked again and desperately searched for a friendly face. This time, she found the gentle giant who smiled at her. Though far away, she heard the gentle giant's stammering voice as she stood up for her and fought against the mob, shouting, "Leave her alone!"

She felt stronger as the gentle giant placed an arm around her shoulder as if to say, *No one can hurt you now*. The gentle giant's arm allowed the girl to mentally recede into the background. It gave her permission to maintain her place outside the body. The torturous chant now seemed to come from far away. How could that be? Her body stood front and center before the mob, but she was not present. She watched them heckle her. She felt them push her body. She heard them yell and mock her body. They did not realize she was not present. They laughed, accused and shamed her. She observed it from a great distance. She observed it from her place of safety. She had done it before, but this was the first time she became profoundly aware of her capacity to spiritually protect herself by disconnecting completely from her body and rising above the fearful moments. This young girl was me.

That day I was wrongfully accused of being a lesbian. I

was mocked and tortured verbally for being in a same-sex relationship with one of my peers. At that stage of my life, I did not know who or what I was. I felt very lonely, like a lot of the other students. I was also younger and less mature than most of my peers. I formed bonds with a lot of students — my peers, my seniors and my juniors. I do not know how the rumour started, but it took a life of its own. That day, I was transported to hell and back. It was a day I would never forget. It was a day that a seed was sown.

Today, I still do the same thing that I did that fateful day. When I entertain, I have an out-of-body experience. I do the same thing when I am giving a speech in front of more than 10 people. I put one foot in front of the other and just keep moving. I say the same things and ask the same questions. I often say, "How are you? Welcome to my home. What do you do? I am passionate about mentoring minority women and children. Do you support any causes? Tell me about your children? We have a Coton De Tulear, it's a Madagascan dog," and so on and so forth. I appear engaged and present, but in reality I have an invisible wall that surrounds me on all sides and announces, "Don't come near me. Don't hurt me." I protect myself the same way I protected myself on that day so long ago.

Fog

I have always seen myself on stage, but it never materialized until adulthood. I may never know why. I rely always on the biblical promise that all things happen in the time and season preordained by God. Maybe this is my season. The season took very long to materialize, and is a fruit of lots of joyful and painful experiences.

It took a while for me to recognize that spiritual separation from my body did not begin with the trauma inflicted by those students. It began at age six when the darkness of sexual assault entered my life. My childhood is painted with dark colours of sexual abuse, which was made bearable because I had a loving family. A loving but unaware family. They had no clue what happened to me. My privileged upbringing helped distract me, but only marginally.

My parents fled from our home country Nigeria to Ghana because of a senseless war that broke out and resulted in the deaths of over one million people. My father was a doctor and my mother was a teacher. When the war broke out, my father, mother and brother were living in Lagos. I was in my mother's belly. My mother tells the story of how they were told to leave Lagos because everyone of Ibo extraction was going to be killed. My father went to the British embassy to apply for a visa but was turned down because the Nigerian "quota" was exhausted. The embassy official advised my father to go to Ghana because "it's easier to get a visa there." This began my family's journey to Ghana, where I was born.

It was in Ghana that I was sexually abused by a man, who in my six-year-old eyes, looked like a giant. My abuser was the house help. He looked after the house when my parents were out. I do not remember how he had access to me, because I also remember that we had a female nanny who looked after us when my parents were at work.

My abuser personifies everything that I am scared of in my life. The bogeyman hiding under my bed or in the closet at night. The car jacker who I imagine shooting me when I stop at a traffic light. The death of my loved ones. The end of my marriage. The rejection by people I love. The lack of affection from my partner. The absence of an arm around me to protect me. My anxieties. My worries. My failures. He represents them all. When these fears rise up, I find myself escaping; I find myself in an out-of-body experience, just like the "Mongoose" day.

I always wonder if my act of retreating was perfected even before the Mongoose incident. Was it a way of protecting myself from the bogeyman who stole my innocence over and over again?

My memories of my childhood are sometimes foggy because I protected myself by disconnecting from my body as the assault took place. I was definitely well provided for by my parents. Lots of love, private schools, around-the-world trips, drivers, gardeners, chefs, nannies, gifts and many creature comforts. I do remember that I had a wonderful 13th or 15th birthday party. I do remember that I had another birthday party, probably my 18th birthday party, where I had my first slow dance with a friend of mine, who remains a very dear friend and confidante to this day.

Unfortunately, my upbringing created opportunities for me to operate at a level that exposed me to men and women who were entitled and believed that it was their right to lust after me and, in some cases, violate me. I sometimes wonder if I unconsciously enticed them. Am I to blame because I was given a body that as my best friend once said, "screams sex"? I loved my body because it was a currency. I hated my body because it was a currency.

I Deserved It

I spent a lot of my elementary school years in a cyclical, abusive environment. Male servants, drivers, cooks and my male cousin preyed upon me. I felt like I deserved it, and in some cases, I sought them out by going to the boys' quarters to engage them. I fantasized about intercourse with some of them. I encouraged them to continue to abuse me. It was yet again an out-of-body experience. I always found myself not really comprehending what I was doing in the moment. I would hate myself after every encounter, and the hatred increased each time. I was not even a teenager. They were all at least 20 years old or older.

High school was a defining moment for me in a lot of ways. I was quiet but popular. I was unsure of myself but somehow got grouped with the "cool and sometimes bad group of kids." In high school, I started to make up stories about an imaginary set of twins that I met on a flight to America. My friends lapped it up, so I made up more lies about them. I also sought attention in crazy ways — I started to cut myself. I also started to pretend that I was losing consciousness. I always felt the need to leave my body to escape. I was always leaving or running away so that I could protect myself. To leave was to create a safe boundary for myself. I would see myself cutting myself and view it as someone else.

Eventually, I was sent home from boarding school on sick leave. My father sent me back with the words, "I know there is nothing wrong with you." I just planned more ways to get attention. These included imaginary love affairs with any gender. I did not know what it meant. I did not act it out then. I just imagined it.

Movie Script

University was my first foray into the world of adultery. I was a Christian and fornicating. When you add a married man to that equation, it becomes adultery. So, while I fell in love with this man, it was bittersweet because I was always worried that my parents would freak out if they knew (plus God was watching). Academics came second because my focus was on this unhealthy relationship. I was 18 when I met him and he was 34. The way we met would make a good scene for a movie script.

My mother took me to the airport to catch a flight. The coach section was full, so she bought me a first-class ticket; it was a ticket that saw me sitting next to this dashing, tall man who spoke so eloquently, and when he laughed his eyes twinkled. He had me as soon as he said, "Is this seat taken." We talked throughout the two-hour flight. He understood me. Ironically, I saw him as my protector. He was going to protect me from the big bad wolves. I was always in a flight mode and I felt that I needed a saviour. That was the beginning of the end for me.

My grades suffered as I dated him throughout university. The relationship was exciting. Secretive nights at his house, away from the university campus. Heartache when he briefly dated someone else because I was behaving like a spoilt brat. Ecstatic joy when we got back together. Fear and disappointment in myself when someone told my parents about the relationship. The relationship went beyond my undergraduate days, ending only when I met a young man who took my breath away emotionally and physically.

I barely came out of university with a 3.33 GPA. I did not realize the impact of this until I applied, unsuccessfully, for a Ph.D at a North American university. My GPA was not the only reason for being turned down but I believe it played a role. I recognized that my lackadaisical approach to education had set me on a challenging path.

My post-university days were also interesting. I was a voluptuous lady (also known as curvy in today's politically correct world). I had two postgraduate degrees, one from a Nigerian university and another from a North American university. Graduate school in the Nigerian university saw me getting a lot of attention because I was a very comfortable student. My social life vacillated between the student events and the non-student, or "town" events, as they were called. The use of "town" had a scandalous undertone. It was synonymous with having a "sugar daddy." If you party with the "town" crowd, you must be a kept woman, regardless of whether this is true or not.

I met a great guy while I was in graduate school. It was a fun and highly sexual relationship. I had a romantic, butterfly-in-my-stomach feeling. Despite this, I always felt like I had to prove something. I always felt that I was less than enough. My out-of-body experiences continued and were now a way to mask my low self-esteem. I did not feel that I deserved to have a great guy. I felt dirty because I was a sexually abused female, adulterer, mistress and a woman with no real passion about anything. I was 23 years old and doing an MBA, and yet I still felt less than adequate. I felt that I had to prove myself. I felt that I had to shout louder than others to be heard. I felt that the bogeyman was there in the shadows and stifling my soul.

I became very angry and it showed. I became self-destructive. I sabotaged myself time and time again. I was destroying people I met with my words, systematically but surely. I was destroying myself with my thoughts of self-doubt. I was sweet on the outside, and bitter and scathing on the inside. My thoughts were evil. My actions were somewhat depraved. Alcohol and sex became my escape. Yet, I still felt like all of this was not me. I felt like I wasn't the one doing all of this. I felt like I was watching someone else's life unfold before my eyes. It was me and at the same time, it was not really me.

At the end of graduate school, I woke up one morning to the sound of knocking on my apartment door. It was my father's driver. He had been instructed to take me back home, as my father had got a job for me at his friend's bank. I was devastated because I fancied myself getting a job in the town I was in, so that I could be near my boyfriend.

Despite my pain, I packed up and off I went to start my new life. I grew up in a culture and time when your father's word was law. As the driver pulled away, I could see nothing past the tears that were welling up in my eyes.

It transitioned to a long-distance relationship, fraught with difficulties but we persevered.

Stages of Life

I believe every human being goes through defining moments in their life. In the course of writing this chapter, I have started to look at my life stages like that of a butterfly.

On one hand, my larva stage was full of warmth, love, favour and blessings, and on the other hand it was dark. I was supposed to be a child, simply playing, eating and growing. I was transported beyond my years by the darkness of sexual abuse.

My pupa stage is where I started the art of performance. This was need based — the need to protect myself from the hurt of sexual abuse. I am very empathic and compassionate. I have strong emotional intelligence. I find joy in doing for others. I get satisfaction by giving back. I almost always root for the underdog.

I had all of these great qualities to build upon, but I chose to ignore them and focus instead on being self-destructive and angry. I always found fault with others. I was upset about everything. I was rude. I was caustic. I was arrogant. I felt the world owed me something.

Frankly, after the sexual abuse and the public shaming, I felt entitled in my anger. The curious thing was that I did not realize that my bad behaviour was due to the abuse and the public shaming.

I just knew that I was always angry and combative.
I was always tense.
I was always absent and continuously leaving;
I was never staying.
I was never mindful of my surroundings or my actions in the moment.
I always regretted my behaviour, but I could not stop myself from being self-destructive.

I walked into a room as if I owned it. I swayed and sashayed knowing everyone was watching and lusting. I loved the stage I created for myself.

Outside, I was confident and borderline arrogant.

Inside, I was shaking like a leaf because I was not sure if I was good enough for them to like me.

Throughout my life God has blessed me and opened doors for me in ways that I did not need to compromise myself. However, in my self-destructive way, I found myself compromising myself anyway. Because I was not mindful and I almost always left, I was never able to turn my blessings into the kind of success people only dream about.

In recent years, I went into a period of true self-reflection. A period I call my Pre-Butterfly stage. I acknowledged my experiences, feelings, strengths, weaknesses, victories, failures and my desperate need for help. I tried self-help books, biblical seminars, spiritual books, Bible studies, prayer, fasting, and so on. There seemed to be an improvement, but a small incident would send me spiraling out of control. I would pick myself up and start all over again. This cycle happened so often that I became weary.

From time to time, I began performing on my self-appointed stage. I would do it informally in my home while entertaining, or formally in front of over 50 women. I found that speaking my truth was therapeutic for me. People found it inspiring and helpful. I was able to self-reflect.

I came to a conclusion that I knew was coming. I sought help and I began therapy (individual therapy and group therapy). I was diagnosed with ADHD and general anxiety disorder. I found my voice. I found my true self. Now, I am in a better place. I can view things from a balanced perspective. I developed my wings. Wings that get cut from time to time but they are my wings, not the wings of my alter ego or my out-of-body self. They are all mine.

I am doing the work I need to do. I have remembered and forgiven things that I needed to. I know my triggers now, and I can remain in myself and say no. I have created boundaries. I am in the present and there is no need to be fearful.

My butterfly stage is a beautiful place to be. I am not a perfect butterfly, but I employ my mindfulness practice. I use my meditation. My family grounds me and my God is my anchor.

I am Ajua Phillips

My purpose is to empower others, not change them.
My purpose is to speak my truth, not impose my truth on others.
My purpose is to know and serve my God intimately, not impose religion on others.
My purpose is to be joyful, not to brood.
My purpose is to make a quiet but impactful mark on the world, not suck up all the air in the room.
My purpose is to strut my stuff and teach others how to do the same as they journey through life.

CHAPTER 5

The Return Home

I AM Rayna Hilary

Between Sept 2015 and March 2018 I experienced two accidents that left me with a concussion and significant physical and mental impairments. I was struggling and I decided that there had to be more to life than just existing. I was on a quest to improve my health and I sought out the help of a transformational therapist and together we embarked on a forgiveness journey that changed my life.

After moving through the forgiveness journey, I experienced a deep connection to myself and God than I had ever felt before. Within days there was a spark of creativity welling up inside me that was tangible. I felt excited and so alive when I woke each morning. I no longer had to drag myself out of bed, but waited with anticipation for daylight so I could begin my day.

Realizing my destiny and true purpose in life followed shortly after, and I haven't looked back since. I have had a few challenges in my life, but now I am experiencing freedom! Free to soar and be the woman God had always intended me to be. I am full of joy when I say there is a deep level of harmony, peace of mind and fulfillment that comes with forgiving the people who deeply wounded me. I am now my true self and living out my destiny. If you are not already at this point in your life, please come with me on the forgiveness journey and walk in the love and light that Christ came to shine in and through us.

My sixth birthday was a sunny, brilliant day. My mother had bought me the most beautiful pink-doll birthday cake. It filled me with happiness and excitement as I looked at it. I don't remember anything else about that day, but it is a lovely memory. I have other memories of my childhood but some of them are not pleasant. I wish to take you through some of my experiences, in the hopes that telling my story will help someone else in their life journey.

At six years old I was sexually molested for the first time. Unfortunately this was not to be the last time, and after that there were other similar incidents that spanned many years. I was abused over and over again by three different men and one of their sisters. This left me withdrawn and twisted in a ball of pain. I could not understand why this had happened. What had I done to be harmed and treated this way? I felt unloved, unprotected, scared, angry towards men, and I blocked out the flashbacks to cope. I struggled through many turbulent years in my childhood.

At 10 years of age, my mother met a man who later became my step father. He and I had lots of conflict over the years. In order to deal with our difficult relationship, my coping mechanisms involved withdrawing into myself and filling my heart with rebellion. My parent's relationship was volatile at times, and they argued quite often. They both came from dysfunctional homes and they repeated the same patterns that were taught to them.

When I was 13, my parents decided we would move to another province for my step father's new job.

I felt as though my world had been turned upside down. The thought of moving away from my best and only friend bothered me. I devised a plan to run away from home so I would not have to move with my parents.

As the moving date got closer, I decided it was time to execute my plan. I packed a bag and made my preparations. I had no plans of getting caught or ever coming back, and figured making it on my own had to be better than my situation at home. To my surprise, I was found by the police within hours of running away, and my parents picked me up and took me home.

If I thought my home situation was bad before, now it was like being under house arrest. The rejection and anger from my mother and step father were evident in their interactions with me. I now experienced a deeper form of loneliness and despair than ever before. I felt completely alone, and a few weeks later we moved away.

The move came with its own set of challenges. I hated where we moved to and the private school. I missed my best friend and I had no one to talk to. At our new church, my mom confided in a woman about my past. This woman also worked at my school. My mom told her about me running away, and this woman decided to share this information with other people. I wasn't given a fair chance after that, and I was always watched very closely. I felt like I was always under a microscope. That was the final straw; my heart broke. Even strangers were passing judgment before getting to know me. Couldn't anyone see my pain and the heart break in my eyes? Could the world really be this cold and heartless? My only answer was yes.

Rules and indoctrination in the name of religion were now part of my daily training and education at my new school and church. There was little mention of the power of the Holy Spirit or how much unconditional love God had for me. It seemed to me that all I learned about were endless dos and don'ts. I am a sensitive soul; all I longed for was to fit in and be accepted. My heart ached for someone to truly accept and care for me. I did make one dear friend and she was smart and fun. We spent as much time together as possible, and I believe she helped me maintain my sanity during that time.

After five years of enduring life instead of enjoying it, I left home again on my 18th birthday. I wrote a note and left the province. This hurt my mother deeply.

The beginning of my adulthood was shrouded in a series of poor choices. I had run off as fast as I could into the real world, but my toolbox was missing the necessary tools to succeed. Without good advice and support to guide me, I was unprepared for what lay ahead in my future. Not to mention by this point I could have really used some serious therapy and counselling to begin the healing process I so desperately needed.

I have heard other women say, "What is it about me that attracts these predators?" I would also like an answer to that question. Do we exude vulnerability or fear? Whatever it is, it soon attracted the next person to take advantage of me and abuse me. At work, my boss began making sexual advances and I felt completely trapped. Soon he began taking the liberty to repeatedly force himself on me. I had no will to fight and I didn't want to lose my job, so this went on for months. Fear and anger gripped my heart like never before. Why couldn't anyone see the special person I was? Why did they only come to violate me, use me and then leave? My experiences taught me some lessons. They shaped and changed how I viewed the world.

I began to believe that you should never trust anyone unless you want to be disappointed. People only want to use you and throw you away when they are finished with you. Life can be very cruel, and when your back is against the wall it is likely no one will come to your aid.

At the age of 19, I caught the eye of a guy at the gym. Up to this point I thought I had learned some hard life lessons, but I wasn't prepared for what this man was going to bring into my life. He was a "player" who was 15 years my senior. He swept me off my feet, with smooth words and flattering gestures. He brought me flowers at work once, took me away on weekends, and gave me the time and attention that I had never experienced. I felt like I was walking on air; someone was genuinely interested in me, or so I thought. Little did I know, much of what he said to me were boldfaced lies. He lied about his age and marital status; he had already been married twice and had many children.

One fateful morning I answered a knock at my door. I opened it to see a woman standing there. She kicked the door in, and it hit me in the face. My boyfriend, hearing the commotion, came to the door to see what was going on. The woman began screaming and tried to hit me. He got in between us and separated her from me. I stood there, stunned, and it became clear to me that this was his wife. I was quite shocked because he had recently proposed marriage and I had accepted. I did not know that he was already married. As the two of them continued to argue, they moved outside to the front of the house. It was then that I heard a loud crash. I ran outside and saw that she had crashed her car into his car, the car in my driveway and was now reversing into the road. She saw me come out of the house and drove straight towards me. I attempted to run but slipped on the grass that was wet with morning dew; it sent me flying to my knees. The pain seared through one knee and then the other. I have serious knee issues to this day.

I broke up with him that day but he didn't want to leave. He eventually left, but came back later to say we were not breaking up and that he was in love with me and not her. After that I tried to avoid him for days and planned to leave town if that's what it took to be free of him. While I was arranging to leave, he began pursuing me like never before and slowing but surely he weaseled his way, back into my heart.

He told me this time would be different because he was so in love with me and he had changed. Sadly, I began to believe his lie. Please don't be fooled by such lies if they are told to you. You can avoid making some of the mistakes I made. Read the signs, and if your gut keeps telling you something isn't right, it usually isn't. I'm not saying people can't change, but if their life pattern is a certain way, there is a good chance it will continue in that pattern without God's intervention. I decided to let him back into my life and we dated for a while before getting married. By this time I had reconciled with my parents, so we went to see them and get married there.

The day before the wedding, I decided to tell my mother about the sexual abuse I had endured as a child. I felt I needed to get it off my chest before I got married. She was devastated. Despite the gravity of the situation, I felt a tiny bit better because at least now I had acknowledged it to someone else. It was finally out in the open after so long.

We went to the Caribbean to visit my husband's family. I fell in love with the peaceful lifestyle and we decided to move there. The move was quite an undertaking but together we completed the task, and it drew us even closer together. I felt like I was in a fairy tale; my life was finally fantastic! I had a nice husband, beautiful dream home, awesome climate and the beach. Things had sure turned around! I wondered how life could start out so rough and now be so right, but I wasn't going to question it. I loved my life and I felt content.

As I mentioned, my husband had many children before our marriage, so I was hesitant to have children with him. I worried that he would do to me what he had done to other women. Also, my father had never raised me as his child and I didn't even know him, so I wanted to make sure that if I had children with my husband, he was going to stay around and be a father to them. I believe children grow up best with both parents in their lives, if that is possible.

Two years after moving to the Caribbean I went off the pill for health reasons, and was surprised to get pregnant almost immediately. After getting over the initial shock, I was very happy. We were both excited! We had a beautiful baby boy, and all was right in my world.

A few days after coming home from the hospital, a man came to our house. He asked to speak to me and told me my husband had been having an affair with his girlfriend. I asked the man to leave and he did. I confronted my husband about it, and he denied it. A tiny seed of doubt began to grow in my gut. You know the place, where you get that feeling that something isn't quite right? I later found out it was indeed true.

The doubt soon gave way to my strong desire for a happy and unified family, and I wanted that more than anything else. Life ran smoothly for a while, but the rumours of my husband's infidelities grew at a steady rate until denying them wasn't really an option for me. As much as I wanted to ignore them, they were not going away. People I knew began to speak freely with me about what they had seen or heard about my husband. I questioned their motives but realized there was just too much to ignore anymore. During our marriage he had multiple ongoing relationships with other women.

Four years later, we decided to have another child. My desire for a second child came from my own personal experiences. I was an only child and growing up I had been lonely. I didn't want that for my son. By the time our second son was born, things between my husband and I were even more strained. We spent very little time together and our relationship began to unravel. I decided that after almost 10 years of his cheating, maybe he would change if he got a dose of his own medicine. What a ridiculous thought! I had an affair, but the guilt was almost unbearable, and it haunted me to my core. How could I, as a believer, have stooped so low? He knew about the affair and said, "We could stay together and keep the other people in our lives."

He was fine with it, but I was devastated. To top it all off, the girl he was seeing was young enough to be his daughter, and that made me sick. My foolish plan had backfired, and I had done the very thing that I never dreamed I would do. Who had I become?

One evening, I decided not to come home. The next morning, we had a big argument. He was furious and walked away, and I thought that was the end of the argument. Then I heard this loud banging sound, and I looked over at the staircase. He was coming up the stairs, smashing a machete on each step. I turned and ran in fear. Something inside me said, "Stop, don't run. If you do, he will hurt you." So I stopped in the family room and waited for him, and as he approached, I began to pray. I asked God to protect me and not let my husband hurt me, and after a few minutes he turned and walked away.

After that day, I moved out with our sons. The only place I could get quickly wasn't in the greatest of neighbourhoods, and within a few short weeks of us living there, our apartment was broken into and everything of value was stolen. We could not continue to stay there; it wasn't safe for us. We moved back into our home, and my husband lived in a separate part of the house from us. This went on for many years until the house sold. It was so disturbing to see everything we had built together fall apart, and I was deeply wounded. Knowing our sons would grow up without a father and mother together in the home, tore me apart inside. The very life I had tried so hard to avoid was now our reality.

There was a shift in my heart after that. I had prayed to and loved God, tried to be a wonderful wife and mother and this was the reward? Maybe God didn't love me like I thought He did? Maybe He wasn't interested in my life as I had previously believed. My heart grew cold.

After the house sold we moved to the city where I began pursuing a career in fashion design. It was a passion of mine. I also wanted to show my ex-husband that I could accomplish something great and make him regret what he had thrown away. I enjoyed the fashion world and with a lot of hard work, my designs started to get noticed. A few celebrities purchased pieces and I was quite excited! A bit of my self-confidence was restored; it had been almost demolished along with my self-esteem. Life started to make sense again and I was a bit stronger.

I had always wanted a daughter, and with my heart still hardened against God I continued to pursue my own plans. My biological clock was ticking, and I knew I didn't have much time left. In selfishness I decided I would have another child, and it would be with someone who understood that this would be my child, not his. There would be no fight over my little one, no family court, nothing. I put my plan into action and got pregnant.

When I went for my first ultrasound, they saw a tear in my womb, and told me that I probably wouldn't be able to carry this baby to term. I left there with faith, determination and plenty of prayers that I would carry this baby to term. I took precautions and had plenty of bed rest, with my feet elevated as much as possible. Around a month and a half before my delivery date, I had another complication. But in the end out came this little cherub. A day or two later I went home with my beautiful bundle of joy! She was the most beautiful baby girl I had ever seen.

My heart began to soften because God had been so merciful to me, giving me two wonderful sons and the gift of this little girl. I was truly grateful! Many people may disagree, but I felt my daughter was God's special gift to me. God had seen all that had transpired in my life and granted this gift in spite of my many mistakes. It warmed my heart.

When my daughter was around one-and-a-half years old, I began feeling God touch my heart about returning to Canada. I prayed about this matter over and over again. I didn't want to go back; I loved the warm weather and my friends, and my career was starting to take off. Going back would feel like failure and I wanted to stay. Finally, after close to a year, I came to terms with going back and began making the plans. Even though I had prayed so hard about going back, I didn't pray about where to go in Canada. I felt the only place to go would be the same city as my parents. This would make them happy even though I didn't like the place. I had their only grandchildren and I felt obliged to go there.

My oldest son who was 15, decided to stay with his dad to finish school. So, my second son, 10 years old, daughter, two-and-a-half years old and I travelled to Canada, to start our lives over. Not long after moving back to my parents' hometown, I regretted my decision; this wasn't the place for us. I felt my parents still treated me like I was 14, except now I was a grown woman with children. I began praying and asking God where He wanted us to go and asking His forgiveness for not asking that question in the first place. After a lot of prayer, I felt I had the answer. We left at the end of August after having spent a little over a month with my parents.

I moved to a small town in southern Ontario. I rented a place from a woman who I had known before I had moved to the Caribbean. After moving in, I noticed that there was a church within walking distance from where we lived. We attended it and immediately I noticed that the people were very friendly, genuine, caring and non-judgmental. They were very different from the people in the church I had been raised in.

One Sunday, I was approached by woman and she asked if I would like to go for coffee sometime. We set a date and met the next week. She was so sincere and kind, and we became good friends. There were many other friendships that blossomed here for both me and the children.

I began learning about the power of the Holy Spirit and how God loved me unconditionally. It was a spiritual process and one that is still taking place in my life today. I am so grateful to these people who showed me a new way to have a deeper relationship with God. This was the beginning of a beautiful transformation!

We began to really become settled in our new life. Home life and work continued as usual until one day I was working a holiday shift. I walked into a walk-in freezer to get something and before the door shut fully behind me, I slipped. Both feet slipped in opposite directions and before I knew what had happened, I was doing the splits. The pain was beyond belief; it burst through my body. To make a long story short, a few days later I received some very distressing news and felt something else happen to my body. The right side of my body became temporarily paralyzed, and on the way to the hospital, I lost the ability to speak for a short period of time. These symptoms corrected themselves within minutes, but in the following days I realized that my short-term memory was severely affected. I couldn't remember the simplest of things.

Tests were run and they found that two arteries in my neck had blocked. I was so concerned about this unfortunate turn of events that I went to my church for healing prayer. The next test results found that these arteries were no longer blocked. Thank you God! Despite this relief, I knew my short-term memory was no longer functioning correctly. Walking was extremely painful, but I still needed to take care of my dear children as best as I possibly could.

The next few months were very challenging. We had to move from where we lived, because I no longer had an income. A dear friend offered to rent us an apartment and he was willing to work with me concerning the rent payments. My church and friends assisted me financially; it was remarkable to experience God working through people to help me, when I was unable to help myself. My slipping injury still affects me and I have almost constant neck pain. My short-term memory is still somewhat impaired more than four years later. However, I am so grateful to God and all those who helped us, and for my healing that has occurred. God does work miracles, sometimes big and sometimes small!

The next few years were more difficult than I could have ever anticipated, but I turned to God for strength and guidance. After moving from the Caribbean, I had dated a bit but Mr. Right did not come along. I was disillusioned with the whole dating scene. I finally just gave up and asked God to bring the man straight to my door if he wanted someone in our lives. It weighed heavily on my mind that my children were growing up without a father figure that they so badly needed.

My dearest friend in the Caribbean asked a close friend of hers to pay me a visit. We had a great visit, and he thought I was an awesome person. After our visit, he told his best friend about me because he thought we should meet. It took many months and a few meetings that didn't materialize before we finally met. The day arrived that we were supposed to meet and we chose the meeting place.

He was running behind schedule and gave me a call to explain that he was going to be late. I told him no problem and to text me when he was closer. I was not concerned; this was just some friend of a friend. If we didn't get to meet, it was no problem.

The day progressed into the late afternoon and I was getting ready to bring a chocolate fountain over to woman for her birthday party. I had to be there in approximately 35 minutes when the phone rang. It was him and he was close by. I felt so bad. He had driven for over two hrs to see me. I did not have enough time to finish getting ready, reach our meeting place and ensure that the chocolate fountain would reach the woman's party on time. So I gave him directions and told him to pop by.

Not long after I heard a rumbling sound in the driveway. I went out and there he was on a motorcycle. He introduced himself, took my hand in his and placed a kiss on the top of my hand. I felt this surge of energy run through my body from top to bottom. I had never experienced anything like that before in my life. I would never have believed it if I didn't feel it for myself. Was this what people meant when they talked about love at first sight? I felt an instant connection to this man and I stepped back in disbelief. What was happening to me? I had to catch my breath and regain my composure. I asked if he would like to sit for a minute, and he said yes. So we went and sat on the back veranda and talked for a bit.

I looked at my phone to check the time and realized I had to go. I turned to him and said, "Why don't you come with me while I set up the chocolate fountain I have to deliver?" He agreed with a smile and we left together. At the party, I went inside and he stayed outside with the other guests. Suddenly, he came in and said that he had set up the fountain. I finished melting the chocolate, poured it into the fountain and it was perfect. The guests loved it and it was a great success!

He stayed close by me for the remainder of the evening and I loved his company. I felt as though I never wanted the evening to end. Other partygoers asked for an introduction to him and I found myself wishing I could say he was my other half. In the following months we got to know each other better and began spending a lot of time together.

As we got to know each other more deeply, I learned more about his life experiences. I learned he had been in a series of accidents and had frontal lobe brain damage. This affected him in similar ways to my injuries. This was something that brought us closer together since we were able to understand each other and share in our experiences. We eventually became a couple, and are happily together today.

I can see now that my injuries have given me more understanding and empathy than if I had not experienced them. This taught me that many of our worst moments in life can be used to help and comfort others, if we allow God to work in our hearts. If you add up childhood trauma, turbulent home life as a teenager, a dysfunctional adulthood, broken marriage, and other unpleasant experiences, you can see that I had a lot of baggage. I had to surrender all of this to God and allow Him to heal the broken and shattered parts of my life. This was not instantaneous, and the healing continues within me every day. I have also seen tremendous growth in the life of my parents; God has done a beautiful work in their marriage.

Today, we have a healthier relationship and I am grateful for that. I have found that forgiveness is a key element in the healing process. Learning to forgive yourself and others who deeply wound you is a crucial step. Once I took the first steps to forgive, I felt a wholeness I had not felt before. I believe it is an ongoing process until our days are done on this Earth.

My forgiveness and reconciliation journey took place on multiple levels. I had to forgive myself. Regret and guilt for past mistakes had me feeling trapped, so I acknowledged that I felt that pain and forgave myself. Allowing forgiveness to be a regular occurrence in my life has encouraged my personal growth. Forgiving others has given me peace of mind and a deep inner healing. When forgiveness becomes entwined within our daily lives, we become healthier and stronger individuals. My relationship with God is stronger and deeper also.

Who I am now is someone who is transforming from a damaged individual to God's daughter with a purpose. My purpose is to forgive whenever it's needed and to love those in my life deeper than they have been loved before. I strive to be someone who is kind and more thoughtful than I was in the past, and I aspire to be a virtuous woman. I fail many times, but this is not where I will remain. My lifetime experiences have challenged me to treat others as I would like to be treated. There is a destiny and a plan for my life and my family, of this I am sure. I am grateful to God for the opportunity to live, love and care for others as He unfolds more of His purpose and plan for me!

CHAPTER 6

Pain To Purpose

I AM Daniella Parlane

"It wasn't a walk in the park," I say as I stare intently into my red cup filled with espresso. A knot forms in my stomach as I force myself to swallow. The brown foamy beverage I usually look forward to has lost its appealing taste. "If there is any way I can prevent another woman from going through what I've experienced, then I am okay with having lived the nightmare." My friend and I exchange that look that women exchange when they connect deeply. She wants to know what has changed. She wants to know why I refuse to stay silent anymore. She has been waiting for this moment for years.

"Look at you, getting all brave on me. You look determined. You look happy. It must be your knight in shining armour and those three beautiful kids . . ." she says. Her voice trails off and I know what she wants to say but she is too kind to say it. I think it all the time. She wants to know why I let the suave Cuban mess me up. I used to ask myself this question, but it's not the right question to ask anymore. My life is not about pain anymore, it's about purpose.

If I could go back in time to warn the younger me, would I? I'd like to think so, but if it altered where I am right now and what the journey ahead is all about, I'm not sure I would change a thing. I am here to help the broken-hearted 16-year-old, the woman struggling with that suffocating marriage, and the woman whose life is torn to pieces by divorce. If I gave up my past with the Cuban, how could I do that now?

Broken Beginnings

I was raised in a Christian household, which I am eternally grateful for. I received an abundance of knowledge about Jesus, attended church regularly and had a general grasp of the gospel. However, I believe I began to gradually loosen this grasp when "life happened." I have flashbacks of my parents arguing. I remember the nights I buried my head in my pillow to block out the yelling. They were not happily married, and this was reflected in everyday life. My father was emotionally unavailable, and my mom overcompensated for this. My young mind subconsciously absorbed this way of life, and it gradually shaped my views and expectations as I developed into a young woman. It was no surprise when, in my late teen years, my parents eventually divorced. This critically skewed my perspective on God. It left me with an enigma. The God I was being taught about was this unconditionally loving God who was all forgiving. Yet, why did my parents' marriage fall apart?

I couldn't reconcile this paradox, so I tried my best to suppress it. At the same time, I was secretly relieved when they divorced because it would finally mean peace for my mom and me. I couldn't stand the fighting. I couldn't stand watching my mom suffer in tears, day after day. I was resolved in knowing that there would be hope in this new beginning — yet the questions gnawed at my soul. Shouldn't Christian marriages always work? Shouldn't there always be a solution? Isn't God's grace sufficient and powerful enough to heal any broken relationship? The questions are still fresh in my mind to this day.

Despite the dysfunction that was occurring in my home, I managed to find respite in immersing myself in church youth programs. I found solace in meeting other young people who believed in this God of love. This was my sanctuary. However, I was about to find out how wrong I was. Little did I know that I was soon to experience betrayal and unbearable pain in the very environment that I thought was supposed to shield me from it.

I was about 16 years old and I had never been in a relationship before. I truly wanted to keep myself for a Godly man. This was the way I was raised, and I was going to do the best I could to adhere to this goal. Through my youth group, I met a young man who began to show a romantic interest in me. I noticed his interest in attending church as well as how he pursued me. I was intrigued by this, as well as his ruggedly boyish looks. He was charming, funny and he was a Christian — or so I thought. We eventually began courting and quickly became serious. As we began to spend most of our time together, the time I would invest in spiritual things decreased. I spent less time reading the Bible and more time on the phone. I prayed less and hung out with my new boyfriend more.

I was totally enveloped in this emotional bliss. He was my first love. I wanted him to be the last — and live happily ever after. I was too emotionally high to realize that time spent with him was pulling me further away from God. The thing is, my relationship with God was also an emotional one. It wasn't based on the Word of God. I wasn't rooted. He was more like my personal genie; I rubbed the lamp when I needed something. As a naïve teenager, I was trying to prove to myself that there was indeed such a thing as true everlasting love. I dove heart first into this newfound relationship. He frequented my home daily, but it soon became clear that my father wasn't too keen on him, or the fact that this boy was spending so many hours at the house. This further divided my parents, as they tried to find a middle ground in dealing with the matter. Finally, the ultimatum was given: he was no longer allowed to come over. I was devastated. I wanted so badly to be with him.

My boyfriend was very manipulative. He filled my head with thoughts that pitted me against my parents. Time and again, he pointed out how cruel and heartless they were being. He then pressured me into moving in with his family. In my head, it was like a modern-day Romeo and Juliet scene. I felt as though I had no other choice. I couldn't lose the love of my life. Besides, what did my parents know about love? Their marriage was turbulent at best! I made up my mind, packed up and moved in with him and his family. It lasted eight days. My mom kept calling the house crying and begging me to come home. I couldn't stand the guilt and hearing her sobs on the other end of the line. So, I eventually decided to go back home. It was painful. In the interim, my boyfriend constantly sweet talked me and persuaded me into being physically intimate with him.

"I would never leave you. We will always be together. I am going to marry you," he would say. As much as I tried to resist the promptings not to do it — one thing lead to another — and I eventually gave in. I remember how cheap and broken I felt right afterwards. Guilt and shame. I had a dirty little secret. It didn't help that he began treating me differently — and not in a good way. I felt somewhat violated, but I was still madly in love with him — or so I told myself. Looking back, it was nothing more than an addictive infatuation. I was in love with the idea of being in love.

As time went on, it became painfully obvious that he didn't really have a relationship with Jesus, and this caused my relationship with Jesus to fizzle even further. Church was more of a social club for him, and it was confirmed to me by his family members — none of whom were Christians. I didn't want to believe it. I ignored more red flags and lived in denial, believing that he would eventually change.

He began demanding to hang out with his female friends without me. He started snapping at me all the time and calling me names. "Shut up, you idiot!" he would shout at me. We argued a lot. Our relationship got progressively worse as he became increasingly controlling and possessive. He forbade me from wearing certain clothes and even casually talking to anyone of the opposite sex. However, I was expected to trust him fully. The double standard irked me. It made me suspicious, fearful and insecure. He eventually broke up with me over the phone one day, claiming that things just weren't working out. I will never forget that day. My heart shattered into a billion pieces. Hope, dignity, joy and self-worth crumbled within me. I barely ate for weeks and I lost a lot of weight. I cried for hours on end. I felt like damaged goods and that I was used and disposable. I cried myself to sleep, night after night. I gave him all of me and yet he was ready to break his forever promise and move on without hesitation.

That was when I decided I had enough of Christians. I was filled with bitterness and resentment. I left the church and cut everyone off. I was jaded, to say the least. At the time I needed moral support the most, I refused anyone who tried to offer it. By this time, my parents had also stopped attending church. Their marriage hung by a string. My mom, who I had grown very close to, was the only one who was able to understand what I was going through. We both felt so much pain and disillusionment. Our bond strengthened, but then so did our jaded perspective on God and church.

Over time, opportunities to meet new people arose, and I decided to open myself to the secular world for a change. I figured I'd give dating non-Christians a chance. I needed something fresh, different and real. When I'd hear the word "Christians," I'd cringe and immediately come back with some comment about how hypocritical and bigoted Christians are. I had a terrible attitude and I was a ticking time bomb. But I justified my bitterness on the self-righteous premise that I was still better than they were. I wanted nothing to do with them or their Jesus. The funny thing is that when I think back, I see that He was still surrounding me. He was waiting for me to come back with open arms. God still prompted me — but I hated the gnawing twinge I felt in my spirit, so I chose to ignore it. If only I understood that the conviction I felt was God's love for me. He wanted to protect me and offer me something better. Instead, I interpreted that conviction for condemnation. So, I blatantly rebelled against it, trying to drown out the sound of my conscience. That is when I met the Cuban.

Mr. Suave

I met him through a mutual friend in my second year of college. I started hanging with a new group of Hispanic friends. I was learning Spanish online and the language fascinated me. I was intrigued by this group of friends who were able to engage with me on this new linguistic level. One day he just showed up. There was something about those bold, daring brown eyes and his suave Cuban accent. He was sweet and charmingly shy, but even in those early days a red flag was flying at full mast. My friend warned me right after the introduction that his buddy didn't have good intentions. He was hurting because the mother of his nine-month-old baby had recently died. Yes, the warning signs were present right from the beginning. I ignored my friend and I ignored the feeling in my gut. Denial set in and I assured my friend that I had no intention of getting into a relationship anytime soon — let alone with Mr. Suave. I believed the lie I told him. I just wanted to have some innocent fun with my friends. I embarked on this curious journey of exploration. It was a whole new world for me. A once forbidden territory was now mine for the taking. We started hanging out at pubs, bars, clubs and even casinos. As I spent more time with this group, I noticed that Mr. Suave was showing an interest in me. Then he began pursuing me.

Conviction knocked at my soul, but I continued to plug my spiritual ears. I figured, why not? The "Christian type" wasn't exactly promising. The whole time I was thinking to myself, at least this guy has nothing to hide, and he's certainly not parading in church pretending to be a saint. Little did I know that when a woman feels the urge to start a sentence with "at least" to justify some guy's bad behaviour, there is a billboard flashing the word RUN!

When I think about that time, I'm instantly overcome with regret. I didn't put much stock into the warning his friend offered. I brushed it off. He was much too sweet, and in my mind I wasn't going to get into anything serious. I was just having some innocent fun. Well, a reality check came pretty quickly.

I remember the flashing disco lights. That tight black dress, and my overdone make-up. The fun began losing its innocence as my clothing got tighter and shorter. I certainly wasn't going to be the only nerdy girl on the night scene. The Latin vibes called for a little sass. A sip of rum here and there wasn't going to hurt — I was just loosening up. You know, living a little! A little puff here and there was harmless, right? But the sips soon became gulps and the puffs kept on going. I was living it up. Most of my time spent out with my new friends was in these loud nightclubs. Ear-pounding beats. Flashing, colourful lights. Dancing the night away — with *him*. I did everything in my power to drown out my conscience with the noise. It had become a drug to numb the sharp twinge that tugged at my soul — and it worked pretty well for a little while.

It wasn't long before we became an item. Our relationship consisted of this nightlife, so it remained pretty surface-deep in the beginning. We especially avoided deep conversation because it was too painful. He had lost the mother of his then nine-month-old baby, who was now being raised by his mother. The red flag kept flying steadily. I could feel it, but the rebel in me insisted that I had to hang around. He was broken, and I was going to be the one to fix him. I made the horrible mistake so many women make. The man had become my reconstruction project! If only I had made myself my reconstruction project.

I think about how broken I used to be inside, and even though I couldn't relate to the type of loss he had experienced, I identified with the pain. I was attracted to it, and I wanted to heal him. Also, even though I had told myself that I would not be physically intimate again until marriage — this lifestyle I was involved in wasn't exactly conducive to that. Who was I kidding? I was dating a non-Christian — and a suave Cuban at that. After some time of pretending like it wasn't going to happen, it happened.

When it happened, I felt broken all over again, like I was damaged goods. I had given "The Christian guy" my virginity and now the same feelings had returned. Everything seemed to repeat itself.

Naiveté

Things got serious pretty quickly and the bliss of it all wore off just as fast. I started to notice his hot temper and his trucker mouth. The suave Cuban's charm faded. All of a sudden, he wasn't so shy. His friends' true colours began to show. Their attitude towards women was absolutely lewd. *Bitch. Whore. Bros before hoes.* It was awful. Despite a gnawing at my soul like 10,000 metal claws, I couldn't possibly leave him now. I had fully given myself to him, and in my heart, we were married. I excused his behaviour time and time again because of his horrible past. I felt insecure and not good enough. This only made me try harder.

Then a thought started to nag at me. It dragged me out of my denial. Maybe I was the one who needed to be fixed. Maybe I was the problem. I had committed to being the best partner I could be, and thought that then maybe I'd be good enough. Unfortunately, at 19 years old, I found myself pregnant with his child.

It was a rude awakening for me, but we were going to stick it out and make it work. After all, we were a family now. I thought I was so strong, but every day I felt like a part of me died. His outlook on life was pretty cut and dry: Party. Drink. Gamble. Rinse. Repeat. We had absolutely nothing in common. We fought like cats and dogs. I cried every single day and prayed my unborn child would be born healthy. Meanwhile, his ruthless behaviour became unbearable. He would hurl insults, belittle me in front of our friends, curse me and call me names. *You're nothing but a f--king bitch! You actually think you're funny? You're so stupid! You look like a steam roller ran over your ass!* We brought out the worst in each other. I started to believe what he said about me. Hurting people hurt others. I wish I had understood this at the time! We exchanged the most abominable words. We had horrible fights — even in public! There was lots of screaming, crying, doors slamming and projectiles thrown across the room. As always, it ended with him going out drinking and returning home in the wee hours of the morning, staggering drunk. I can still smell the stench of his breath — beer and cigarettes. It became a way of life.

As the years rolled on by, we would break up and get back together. I can't tell you how many times. I had just about decided that enough was enough, and I broke off the relationship for good — at least that was the plan. During this time, he began pursuing me full force. He called me and cried. He brought me flowers. He became the perfect gentleman, and I wasn't used to that. I remember how I stood my ground and let him know that I no longer had any reason to trust him, but deep within, I was longing to take him back. In the years we had been together, I had tried engaging him in conversations about faith and God, but he avoided them like the plague. He had a very cynical view on God because of the death of his previous girlfriend. But during this separation, he began telling me that our breakup made him reflect on the deeper things in life. He realized what a blessing I was to his life, and that he would be willing to come to church with me if I would only give him a chance. He hit my weak spot and told me everything I wanted to hear. Only God can truly change a person, and they have to want change for themselves first. I learned that the hard way.

We started attending church together, and it wasn't long before he proposed to me. The naïve girl in me wanted so badly for this to happen. I wanted so badly to believe that I finally did it! I managed to fix him. He was now a repented man and wanted not only to invite God into his life, but to also officially marry me. I thought things were finally going to work out, but deep within, the twinge of conviction was flogging me.

Deep in my gut, I knew this was too good to be true, but I allowed myself to get carried away by my emotions and false hope. I was following my heart, just like the mantra I heard time and time again. Follow your heart. If only I had been taught from the start that the thoughts of the heart, the mind and the soul are different. Had I gotten into the Word of God, I would have known that Jeremiah 17:9 says, "The heart is deceitful above all things and it is extremely sick; Who can understand it fully and know its secret motives?"

It took me years to figure out that everything we are taught is just backwards. The heart is connected to our thoughts, which deceive us, and wisdom is connected to the spirit. So much heartache could have been avoided had I just meditated on that one scripture. I had allowed my heart to steer my life, rather than the Spirit of Truth and the Word of God.

I thought things had changed and that our lives together would be so much better. Unfortunately, not long after we were married the charade quickly ended. The church attendance stopped. The bad habits returned. The break ups ensued. Every fresh start offered a new false hope. There was one empty promise after another. I often felt as though I was going insane. The lies, the booze, the gambling, the lashing out, and the clues of infidelity kept on stacking up. We couldn't agree on anything. We had completely opposing ideological views on life. We fought in front of our sweet, terrified little boy. There were times where I wanted to end my life because I hated the person I had become. I was constantly anxious, suspicious, paranoid and bitter. The only thing that gave me a reason to live was that little boy. So, I clung on for dear life and resigned myself to that dysfunctional existence. I believed that this was the cross I had to bear. I thought I deserved it. It was my life sentence, and I was going to have to deal with it for the sake of my son.

Quest for Enlightenment

One night, my husband had another one of his disappearing episodes. I hadn't seen him from 9:00 a.m. until 3:00 a.m. the next day. I had called his phone repeatedly, and I would just get his voicemail. I had left him numerous text messages, and I didn't get a response. I had gotten very frustrated and weary. I still remember the hostility in his voice when he finally answered the phone on my very last attempt. The voice on the other end was slurred. Furious. I simply asked him where he was and if he had been drinking. He immediately snapped at me viciously and threatened, "Yeah, I've been drinking. You don't like it? There's the door! Get a divorce!" That was the day when something finally clicked inside me. He had given me a free ticket out of hell. For the first time, I was overcome with relief. I was totally resolved. I immediately began packing my things, took my son and moved in with my mom. Words cannot begin to describe the peace I felt. I eventually got my own apartment. It was my own little sanctuary just for me and my son. I was now able to delve into my spiritual journey without impediments. There was finally a light at the end of my endlessly long, dark tunnel.

I now found myself on this quest for spiritual enlightenment. The information I was reading up on began to converge with a lot of biblical material. What happened next was almost indescribable. It was as if the words bounced off the pages and came to life. Scriptures I hadn't heard in decades began echoing in my mind. I saw prophetic scriptures linked to current world events. I had to be totally honest with myself in that moment and admit that I needed the unadulterated truth, at whatever cost. I needed to know right then and there: Was God this impersonal energy source or was He the God of the Bible? At that moment, I decided to totally surrender and cry out to God. I cried out to him as the scripture says in Psalm 42:1, "As the deer pants for the water brooks, so my soul pants for Thee, O God." Then Jeremiah 29:14 responded with "And ye shall seek me, and find me, when ye shall search for me with all your heart." It was almost audible when He responded, "Be still and know that I am God." I hadn't heard that scripture in decades, yet here I was, having this surreal encounter with God. He spoke to my spirit.

I began to hear confirmations of that same scripture, Psalm 46:10, on the radio as I flicked through stations on my way to work. *"Be still and know that I am God."* I heard it again on television as I began watching sermons. *"Be still and know that I am God."* I pushed myself to start going back to church, and the pastor preached on the same scripture! *"Be still and know that I am God."* It was surreal! It was like a sharp sword in my spirit. It was more real than anything I had ever experienced. I totally surrendered to Christ at that moment. I gave him the broken shards of my heart and my life. He flooded my soul with a love so deep, I can't even describe it. I had flashbacks of all the moments He was calling me back to Him. He wasn't condemning me. I had been doing that to myself. I was pushing Him away, yet He watched and waited for me to come back to Him.

I often thought about the cross and the fact that He shed His blood for me. He loved me even though I rejected Him for so many years. I begged His forgiveness for so many nights as I cried myself to sleep. I had trouble processing His forgiveness — I couldn't believe He could really love me this much. But each time I asked Him to forgive me, He revealed to me that He had already done it. I just needed to forgive myself. I wanted God so badly and needed Him so desperately. I began reading the Bible every single day. I spent hours seeking Him in prayer and the Bible.

Almost instantly, my desires began to change. I was actually repelled by the very things I once enjoyed. My clothes changed. The music I listened to changed. The things I watched on television changed. Then, it was as if God had given me a glimpse of His heart for people. I would be driving to work and break into tears as I saw the homeless on the side of the street. I could identify with their pain and their need for a Saviour. I had this deep desire to help people like never before. I started evangelizing to my patients at work at every chance I got. I wanted to help every single homeless person I saw on the street, and made sure to share the gospel with them each time I gave them change. The Holy Spirit moved me to speak and do things I would never have imagined. He had given me a new identity. I was no longer that unworthy, insecure woman. My perspective on people changed as well as my views of myself. I was now a child of the King of kings. I was a princess. I vowed to God that I would not enter another relationship if it wasn't His plan. He was going to have to make it extremely obvious.

The void I once had was now overflowing with peace. His grace and His joy was sufficient. I had never experienced this before. People began to see this change in me and even began coming to me for spiritual advice. Friends, co-workers and family members came to me. I had made the decision that I would serve God with every ounce of my being.

God's Sense of Humour

I began participating in different church activities, as well as outreach and mission programs. I wanted to do whatever I could for Jesus. My son was a part of everything I was involved in, given he was only about nine years old when I separated from my ex-husband. I did everything in my power to sow God's Word into Him and wanted to be a role model for him. I began having this strong burden on my heart to volunteer at a food bank or shelter with my son. Everywhere I looked, there was so much red tape involved in having a young child participate alongside me.

One of the many church groups I participated in was a sewing group for missions in Africa. One day, I overheard a conversation a friend of mine was having with another woman in the group. It immediately caught my attention. The room seemed to go silent as I heard the words, "I am volunteering at the food bank with my kids over the weekend." I immediately stopped what I was doing and made sure I heard her correctly.

"Did you say you volunteer at a food bank — with your children?" I asked her. She proceeded to tell me about this food bank that was run by a very small inner-city church.

"They are always looking for help. Why don't you just come one Saturday?" she said with a smile. I was overjoyed!

I showed up the following Saturday, introduced myself and my son, and we immediately put on a pair of gloves and started serving. It was that easy! It was a very small, rundown church in a rough part of town. I eventually transitioned to attending this church since my responsibilities at the food bank increased. There were about 40 members, most of whom were middle-aged and elderly. It was the very last place I could ever imagine finding a husband one day — and I was fine with that. But God had different plans, and a sense of humour!

Shortly thereafter, a young man started attending the church, as well as volunteering at the food bank. I noticed his zeal for God and his amazing voice, as he was frequently asked to lead worship. I was attending prayer meetings every Friday evening, and he was also present. He exuded a passion for God. He was on fire for God, and that was evident. Nonetheless, I didn't feel any particular attraction to him at that point. I simply identified with his spirit.

One day, after serving at the food bank, he approached me as I was mopping the floor. He was a genuinely extroverted guy.

"Hi! I'm Cassidy," he said. "So, what's your story?"

"Where do I begin? Do you have a week?" I responded with a smile. I can still remember his chuckle and the way he looked at me. I gave him a brief synopsis of my life, and he gave me his — which was strikingly similar. A few weeks later, he invited me out for a coffee after one of our Friday night prayer meetings. As we chatted, we were both intrigued by the things we had in common. Most importantly, we shared a passion for serving God.

One day, as we sat in the coffee shop, we noticed a young guy stumbling around and singing at the top of his voice. He was heavily intoxicated. Cassidy beckoned for him to come over to our table. He was holding a paper bag with a bottle of booze in it. We casually chatted with the young man and asked him what he was up to. His name was Andrew. Before long, we began talking to him about Jesus. Cassidy asked him if it was OK for us to pray for him. He began gushing with tears. He told us he had never met anyone who cared for him as much as we did. We asked him if he wanted to accept Jesus into his life, and he said yes in between sobs. Cassidy asked me to lead him into the prayer of salvation that night, and I did. It was a God moment.

As we parted ways with Andrew, he made an interesting comment. "You guys make a really great couple!" he said. As awkward as it made us feel, we understood he was clearly still heavily drunk.

"We're not a couple," Cassidy replied.

"Oh really? Are you serious? I was sure you guys were together," Andrew said.

After Andrew had left, Cassidy walked me to my car. He asked me, "Did you catch what Andrew said? Could there be something here?"

I hadn't thought that far ahead, so I awkwardly responded with, "I don't know."

Soon afterwards, we began talking on the phone daily. More coffee dates ensued. I really enjoyed his company, but still viewed him as a friend. I won't deny that I found him attractive at that point, but I wasn't going to explore the idea that something more could be there until God confirmed it — loud and clear.

One evening in February, I received a call from Cassidy. "Would you like to go out on Valentine's Day? I mean, like on an actual date?" he asked. He kind of caught me by surprise, so I was very cautious in my response. I felt my hands get clammy as memories of my past crept into my mind. It had been about three years since my divorce was finalized. Despite being unprepared for this moment, I agreed to go on a date with him. I then began praying pretty hard leading up to the date. I asked God to reveal whether this date was His will for my life, and if it wasn't, to let it be cancelled.

On February 14th, Cassidy presented himself with chocolates and we had a wonderful date. We danced. We laughed. We genuinely enjoyed each other's company at a deep level. Something clicked that night. Emotions I didn't know I had for him suddenly awakened in me. The physical attraction became obvious, as if a veil had been removed from my eyes. I noticed his chiselled features, glowing chocolatey skin, gorgeous smile, and dreamy brown eyes. *What is happening, Jesus?* For the first time in my life, I knew that I was in love — and it wasn't based on exterior appearances or emotions this time. Those were just an added bonus!

That night, as Cassidy dropped me off at home, he confessed to me that he had suddenly realized he had developed strong feelings for me as well. That was my first solid confirmation — aside from all the other things we had in common. The confirmations just kept on coming as we got to know each other better. God had revealed to me in Deuteronomy 19:15 that "at the mouth of two witnesses, or at the mouth of three witnesses, shall the matter be established." I found this pattern throughout the Bible, and trusted God's Holy Spirit to confirm His will in my life by following this principle. It has never failed me. Just like He had confirmed His identity three times, He would continue to speak to me in the same way. Cassidy experienced the same thing. In fact, he confessed to me that our pastor had previously spoken to him about me. She had suggested talking to me, and that I'd make a good match for him. He shrugged it off at first, but couldn't ignore all the confirmations that ensued after each encounter we had. I also confessed to him that when we attended our church Christmas party a few months prior, my mom said something interesting.

Cassidy had come to the table where my mom, stepfather and I were sitting and introduced himself. The moment he walked away, my mom (who had been relentlessly praying for a Godly husband for me) turned to me and said, "My goodness, that is exactly the type of young man I see as a perfect match for you!" Abashed, I shrugged off that comment.

As time went on, Cassidy and I exchanged more stories like those. We became best friends and have been inseparable ever since. We had perfect peace about this relationship, and we submitted our courtship to our pastors. They blessed us and kept us accountable and in prayer. Those we considered our spiritual mentors also confirmed that they were at peace with our union.

We were married seven months later and I couldn't ask for a better man. It was as if God had custom designed him just for me. God gave me what I needed, not what I wanted. Once I allowed God to show me what I needed, I truly wanted it because my desires became aligned with His. My eyes were opened to the Boaz He put in front of me.

As Cassidy and I embarked on this exciting new chapter of our lives together, we discovered we also shared a passion for writing. God put it on our hearts to write a book together about Godly relationships and marriage, based on all the experiences we had gone through. We wanted to share what God revealed to us individually after mining the scriptures on His design for marriage. Our book *What Love Is Not* was born — followed by two babies, back to back.

We planned our first worship event to launch our book, and we were blown away at the outcome! God then laid it on our hearts to plan a marriage conference, and in that process so many divine connections were made with people who share a similar vision. This is what led us to embark on our ministry "Make Your Marriage Great Again!" We were able to combine all the gifts God put inside us and use them for His glory. God used Cassidy's musical talent, our mutual gift of writing and ministering to people and merged it all together into one amazing masterpiece. I'm inundated with joy as I think about how God used our broken past, our failures and our pain and transformed it into a platform for our purpose: to bring others into the right relationship with Christ, and with each other. If He used me, He can use you.

I AM DANIELA PARLANE.

I am a wife, mother of three, blogger, author and speaker. Today, along with my husband, I've birthed a ministry called "Make Your Marriage Great Again" that resulted from the book we co-authored, *What Love Is Not*. The book was propelled from our strikingly similar experience of failed marriage, and our mutual passion to help others succeed at marriage.

My second book, *Words of a Mute Girl*, depicts my journey with a debilitating anxiety disorder that I struggled with as a child, and how I overcame.

My great passion is to inspire others to have healthy Godly relationships. My husband and I do this through planning and speaking at marriage conferences, seminars, workshops and musical events. My dream is to see many lives impacted across the world through this ministry. www.makeyourmarriagegreatagain.ca

CHAPTER 7

Broken But Not Defeated

I AM Candace Mezetan

My life was perfect. I had everything a little girl could ask for. I didn't know what it meant to feel pain. I didn't know the meaning of emptiness and I never knew that I could lose something so dear to me. Never did I imagine that one wrong turn could impact the future so profoundly.

Growing up, I was oblivious to my surroundings. I lived in a beautiful ranch house located in the heart of the "hood" — Jamaica Queens, NY. The rancid smell of urine permeated the streets, where containers of all sorts decorated the walkways from corner to corner. Gun shots could be heard piercing through the crisp of the night. It wasn't the best place for children to be raised. My house was a rose amongst a bunch of thorns with a red and white veranda; for me this signified love. There was a huge yard that encircled the house. I had my own room with my own TV and I was happy.

I remember swimming in the little plastic pool that daddy bought for my siblings and me. The pool scratched our skin every time we jumped in and waddled out. I remember lying down in that pool pretending I was a great fish in the ocean, flapping my fins vigorously. I remember my little two-piece bathing suit with my little big belly sticking out. I was a plump little girl, with short, picky hair.

I remember the playground set that we had in the backyard. It had swings, and a slide, and a seesaw that my sister and I rode together. Our backyard was filled with rich and green grass; a backyard where vegetables and fruits grew along the perimeter. I remember those days when my sister and I would chase my little brother around the yard, watching him stumble with his chubby legs. I will always hold these memories close to my heart.

I always thought my daddy was a great father based on what he did for my siblings and me. Our family seemed to be perfect, but the truth is while my mom was smiling on the outside and following my father's commands, she was dying on the inside. She lived in agony, working around the clock to paint the facade that we called living. She portrayed my father as the man, the kingly priest of our home for all the world to see. However, there was more to the story.

There were all of these wonderful moments on the surface, but deep within, there was so much pain. Pain that we children never saw; pain that we were too young to understand. She endured physical abuse from the man who was appointed to serve as her protector. She endured mental abuse instead of being showered with praise for her true beauty and worth. She endured emotional abuse as she turned a blind eye to the other women who enjoyed the attention of her husband. She forcefully took on the role of protector, as she shielded us children from the truth. There truly was no happiness or peace.

The innocence that carried me through my early years ended abruptly. At the tender age of six, I became aware of the disharmony. I still remember seeing daddy grab mommy and holding her down as though a prisoner. We stood there in awe, seeing this mighty warrior bring himself to the level of a filthy dog. It was a tug of war, both parents pulling me and insisting that I shadow their being. Mommy's eyes filled with tears and her voice trembled like a sputtering engine. Daddy's stance remained strong and dominant, not touched by fear or emotion. Thunder and lightning raged through our home, weaving from room to room. The rain of fear covered my body.

Mommy called the police, and in the blink of an eye the storm ended. The police advised my mom to leave the house. She was to find a place to go that was away from her unkind, unloving adversary. I turned to take a good look at my protector, the one who called me his Queen, the one whom I called father. My heart began to bleed, and a river flowed from my eyes. The car was flooded as the rivers of my siblings and I combined; our hearts were ripped out and torn to a million pieces. That was the end of daddy. That was the end of our family. Even though we were physically removed from our father, it was he who actually packed up and moved out a long time ago. His abusive nature pushed my mother away. His chronic smoking and excessive drinking made him unfit. All of his yearnings separated him from us. He left us to fend for ourselves.

Changes

After my parents divorced, the bubble I lived in was broken. Life became harder. We no longer lived in that beautiful home. We moved in with my aunt and the new house that we shared with her was cold and unfriendly. There were so many roaches that instead of running from them I decided to befriend them. That way they wouldn't bother me as much. My aunt lived downstairs and we lived upstairs. Our routine turned upside down. My mom worked at night as a United States Postal Service worker. We stayed home during the day, but at night my sister, brother and I spent the night with our grandparents who lived just around the corner.

Suddenly, it happened. There was a new man present in our lives. Would he be the one to turn our grey into sunshine? Would he serve as the new protector and priest of our home? Questions loomed as there was a sense of uncertainty that lurked overhead. My mom needed comfort and love, and this man seemed to fill that emptiness she felt. We didn't see him much, but just enough to know that he was someone significant.

Before we knew it, my mom was pregnant again. In 1990, my little sister was born and she was his child. Where in the world did this man come from? One day I am living with my daddy, and the next day there's a new man in my life. He was tall and very handsome, with dark, deep penetrating eyes. He came to live with us as we continued to live with our aunt. He had an award-winning smile, and had truly won my mom's attention. How? I don't know. Eventually they had a second child together — another girl. Now I had two baby sisters.

Every day we still had to go to our grandparents' house when it was time for my mom to go to work. As I got older, I began to hate going. I hated leaving my two younger sisters behind. I loved them and wanted to stay with them, but we just had to go. Sometimes I wondered why my mom didn't allow us to stay with him at night. She left my two younger sisters with him so why couldn't we stay home too?

Exposed

For a while, there was another person who was staying in my grandmother's home. Her name was Janice and she was my uncle's ex-girlfriend. She was staying with my grandmother because her son had been killed in a gang-related fight. Though she smiled often, her sadness was obvious. I was sure when she returned to her own home in Jamaica, she would sit in her room and cry a lot.

Every night Janice would sit up with me, my sister, and my brother and we would just talk and watch scary movies on TV. During the days and early evenings, she would take us to the store and buy us all the candy that we wanted. She was so nice to us.

One night, while staying at my grandmother's house, I was dozing off to sleep on the couch in front of the TV.

"Candace?" Janice called out from the bathroom.

"Yes?" I answered.

"Can you grease my hair for me?" She asked in a yearning, baby-like manner. She had been busy washing her hair in the bathroom for the past half hour.

"Okay," I replied nonchalantly. I dragged myself over to the bathroom with my feet sliding on the floor. I began to part Janice's hair, and massage the oil into her sparkling scalp. At the age of 10, doing hair was second nature to me. I had tons of dolls that I had given all these fancy hairdos. I even had a doll whose head was detached from her body, but I kept her head because she had lots of hair.

While I massaged the grease into her scalp, I felt Janice's hands grab me from behind. She began squeezing my buttocks, then making her way up to my chest and rubbing the stubs that I had known as breasts.

Oh my gosh...What is she doing? I asked myself.

My mind began to race. This should not be happening. A tingly feeling warped my body and my mind. I felt confused, overwhelmed, stuck and violated all at the same time.

"Jan . . ." I began to say, but she placed her fingers over my lips and pushed her fingers into my mouth. She wanted me to suck them. I began to tremble. I really wanted this to stop. I didn't want to do this. My head began to spin . . . spin . . . spin. I wanted to scream, "I want my mommy!" but no words left my lips. Silent tears ran down my face. Mommy will always make things better. This wasn't right. Something just didn't feel right!

Her hands began to unbutton my pants, and she spread my legs apart. She pushed her finger inside of me. My body tensed up like a frozen ice cube. I had fallen; I had broken.

I can't recall crying out loud, but I must have because the next thing I remember is my grandmother's voice.

"What is going on in there? Open this door right now!" she called from outside of the bathroom door. The intensity of my grandmother's voice shook Janice to the core. She pulled me up from the floor and cracked the door just a little. The next thing I knew my grandmother barged in like a woman with super strength and pulled me out.

Grandma came to my rescue, yet she never said a word. She knew something sinister and evil was going on in that bathroom but she battled it in silence. I followed her footsteps and never uttered a word either. A darkness fell like a blanket over my already battered heart. It affected everything I did. I experienced something no child should go through and it changed me forever.

Janice became a ghost after that night. She immediately left my grandmother's house and I never saw her again. My siblings would ask my grandmother about her. They missed her, but for me, the sound of her name caused me to break down in tears and be overwhelmed with sadness.

Unleashed

In 1994, my mom and stepfather had their final child. My mom continued to work at night, and she apparently felt safe to now leave me and two younger siblings with my stepfather. My new baby brother was the cutest thing that I had ever seen. As my little brother grew, the tensions between my mom and stepfather also grew. My brother had severe behavioural issues characterized by excessive meltdowns, bullying other children and angry outbursts. It seemed at times that my stepfather would encourage this behaviour rather than correct it. They did not agree on much when it came to my brother. Regardless of what my mom wanted, whatever my stepfather said was the law. His favourite quote was "Me run tings . . . tings nah run me . . ."

Even though the family was growing, things were not right. As children, we weren't always aware of what our mom and stepfather were going through. However, in my heart I knew that my mom wasn't happy. I would sometimes see her crying or doing things against her will. Darkness enshrouded our home just as it had enshrouded my life. When things should have been getting better, they were only becoming worse. It soon became obvious that my mom was being physically abused. I remember nights hearing my mom sobbing and whimpering in her room behind locked doors. I remember walking into the kitchen seeing my mom's arm in a twisted hold and she was begging my stepfather to stop. Soon, the abuse became more and more visible and we could no longer deny it. I remember feeling utterly enraged seeing my stepfather abuse my mom.

One day while he was "man-handling" my mom, I boldly looked him in the eye and told him that he was going to go to jail. OH MY GOODNESS! All hell broke loose! He immediately transformed into the Hulk and beat me with a belt uncontrollably. He swung it north, south, east and west. My mother instantly jumped on me as my blanket of protection and together we bore the pain of his anger. Despite the abuse, my mother stayed. Life went on. Our abuse became normal.

Death

It was another one of my step-grandmother's parties. Food, food, food. There was so much to eat, and boy did I eat. I filled my plate with curry goat and white rice and ate to my heart's content. Shortly after eating, I noticed that my skin began to break out with hives. For some reason, I was experiencing an allergic reaction. My legs were welted, and my arms and face puffed up like marshmallows in a microwave. I called home to speak to my mom, but she had already gone to work. My stepfather said, "Come home, I will take care of it."

When I got home, my stepfather said, "Go take a shower and I will put some Dettol on it." He had the right concoction to remedy every situation. I did as he said; I showered, dressed and went to his room. He pulled out his "medicine" and played doctor daddy.

Realizing the severity of the situation, he needed me to take off my clothes so he could rub the Dettol all over my body. His hands were so big and rough. My heart trembled. I felt very uncomfortable and I struggled to stay calm and relaxed. I had to remind myself over and over that it was OK.

"Lay down," he said. He began to rub my legs with the Dettol, maneuvering up towards my stomach. He massaged the Dettol into my pores. He really put his heart into it. He rubbed my arms, bypassed my breasts and then massaged my neck.

Then he stood up and locked the bedroom door.

"Turn over and lay on your stomach," he beckoned

The massaging continued from my neck to my upper back, middle back and lower back; he was pressing deep into the curvature of my spine. He started to rub my buttocks, but it was different this time. It was sexual. Before I even had an awareness of what was happening, he took control. He parted my legs and violated my being. He was so heavy, I couldn't breathe. I was suffocating. I choked on every word that came out of my mouth. Every stroke sent radiating pain all over my body.

I cried. I died. I had no power.

After he was finished, he turned to me and said, "If you open your mouth about this you will DIE!"

What he failed to realize was that it was too late. I was already dead. There was no power left for him to take.

I was overwhelmed with grief. My spirit sunk low, and no one understood why. I sauntered around the house in fear of my life. Night after night when my mommy left for work and the house was fast asleep, he would creep in and violate my being. I couldn't tell anyone. I fell into a secret state of sadness and despair. I felt empty, depleted, unloved and disgusting.

The Bust

I continued to live in a home where abuse was the norm. My mother wore sadness and depression like her daily apparel. She didn't know what to do. She had no one to reach out to. Her own childhood was loveless. She had suffered abuse from my father and now she was suffering abuse from my stepfather. My mother didn't know how to love her children. Her love was expressed through providing — working for what seemed like endless hours. Her love was maintaining a roof over our heads. Her love was ensuring that there was food on the table. A warm embrace or a simple "I love you" was absent.

The abuse we experienced was verbal, physical and sexual. Seeing my sisters get beat would anger me. I wanted to tell my mother so badly what my stepfather had done to me. I started to pray to God that he would leave the house and never return. The ironic thing was that I had a deep struggle in my heart. Despite all that he had done to me, my mom and my siblings, I still loved him. God knew the struggle in my heart.

One day I witnessed my stepfather beating my little sister. I felt so helpless. I was tired of seeing this and I was tired of holding in this secret. If he was going to kill me, he would just have to do that.

I went to my mother to tell her the darkest secret I had buried for so long. I didn't even know where to begin. All I kept thinking was that she wouldn't believe me. Nevertheless, I pushed aside my fear and embarrassment and I told her everything. My mother looked so hurt. I could see the pain and guilt on her face. I realized she blamed herself for this. She immediately called his mother and told her everything. His mother called me a liar. "He would never do something like that!" she said.

His whole family turned against me. My mother and I confronted my stepfather about it and he denied everything. However, later on that day he came clean. He confessed everything that he had done with tears in his eyes. He apologized and begged for my forgiveness. I cried and cried and cried. I looked at him and all I could feel for him was love and compassion. Despite the hurt I experienced, I forgave him. My mom and I were the only two witnesses to this confession. He never admitted this to his family . . . ever.

Change is Going to Come

My stepfather had another daughter from a previous relationship. She was giving her mother trouble, and she came to live with her dad. My mom didn't even know she was coming to live with us. My stepsister now became a target of the beatings and abuse, but for some reason she got it worse than we did. It could have been that she was getting in trouble at school and she had a "potty" mouth that triggered a rage in her dad. Night after night my stepsister got a beating. Her father was always beating her for something. Even minor things caused him to bring a belt to her buttocks. Soon those beatings got out of control and they landed wherever they did; no specific direction. I was praying so hard for her, my mom and for our family. I kept asking God to get him out of the house. I didn't see how this would happen, but it became my daily prayer request.

One day my stepfather beat his daughter so bad that there were marks all over her. He sat on her and whooped her. She was crying, face flushed bright red as she reached out her hand towards me, asking and seeking my assistance. She was longing for me to be her rescuer. All I could do was stand back and cry.

After the tears had died down, we talked. She told me that she could not take these beatings any more. She expressed her anger and desire to kill her father. I spoke to her, calmed her down, and advised her to tell her school guidance counsellor. Whether that was a good thing or a bad thing, it's hard to say. All that I know is that once she told the counsellors, there were investigators coming to our home from time to time to observe and ask lots of questions. These were questions that we were not sure if we should answer or not. In the meantime, we continued living and enduring the beatings and the abuse, starting with my mom continuing down to the children. It was really bad. We were all smiling on the outside and crying on the inside, and the world had no idea of what was going on. Little did we know that our lives would soon change forever.

Jail Bound

It was 3:00 p.m. on a Friday afternoon and there were 15 minutes left until the bell rang. I sat at the drums in band class, making up beats and singing some common gospel tunes that I knew from church. I was in my own little world when two security guards entered the classroom. I didn't really pay them any attention because I never did anything to get into trouble so they couldn't possibly be there for me.

"We need to see Candace Beckford," said the security guard. I looked up startled. They told me to take all my belongings and follow them. We went to the main office and I was confronted with two adults from the Agency of Child Care Services. They looked at me and a young woman pulled me close for a hug. My heart began to race.

"What is going on here?" I asked.

"You see that van outside? All of your brothers and sisters are in that van and we are taking you guys away from your home," she replied. *Away from your home . . . away from your home.* Those words resonated in my head as tears furiously streamed down my face. I felt like a prisoner who was trapped and being convicted even though I did nothing wrong. I felt the glare of students and friends as I was escorted out of the building to the van.

In the van, I saw the gleeful faces of my siblings. I was 14 at the time, and my younger siblings were 12, 10, seven, six and four. My stepsister was in the mix too. They all looked so happy, and that made me cry even more because they had no idea what was going on.

We were taken to the agency where our mom met us in tears. She was crying uncontrollably. She hugged my little brother who was only four years old. We sat and waited around for some news, and soon learned that we were not able to go back to our home. It was deemed to be unsafe.

We were then assigned to different foster homes. We were all getting split up. My three sisters and stepsister were paired off and assigned to two different homes; my two brothers were paired off and sent to a different home. That left me alone. I couldn't believe that this was happening to us. I was petrified! I looked at my four-year-old brother who was happily eating a cookie. He had no idea of what was going on.

My heart was heavy and burdened. I looked at my mom and I could see the sadness painted on her face. After we were assigned to our homes, we had to part from our mother. My heart was bleeding. The pain was immense, and I couldn't escape it. We were all stashed in a van, and we waved goodbye to our mother. She stood there helplessly as my heart broke.

It was a long ride to where we were all going to be fostered. The ride was bleak and silent. No one said a word. All I could hear were the sobs of my sisters over the blaring music. We first stopped in Manhattan, where a physician saw us all. After the checkup, my two brothers were going to be housed in Manhattan and the rest of us were being sent to Brooklyn. My little four-year-old brother waddled over to me with his face hanging low. He cried and asked me not to leave him. He hugged me so tight that I thought I would suffocate. Instead of trying to breathe in a lung full of air, I held onto him too. The facility worker took him and went to give him a bath. He asked me to promise him that I would be there when he came out. I made him that empty promise, just so he would go for his bath. I knew I wouldn't be there. The tears streamed down my face as his eyes locked with mine and he disappeared around the bend. I cried a river as I made my way to the van.

We all went our separate ways. My life was silent in that moment. The next 36 hours seemed like a dream. I tried to push out the fears of never returning home. I tried to ignore my desire to run away from the foster home. Since I was in high school, I was allowed to go to school. I took the train to Queens and I was tempted not to go back, but I had to abide by the rules. I called my mom and told her I was in Queens and she asked me to meet her at the family court.

When we saw each other at the court, my mom hugged me. That was significant because my mom rarely gave hugs. She told me that everything was going to be ok. She had to see a judge and then we would be able to come home. It only seemed like forever, but soon we were able to go home after my stepfather moved out of the house. That was the only way we could be reunited with our mom.

The Planted Seed

Life continued, but it was filled with an emptiness and a longing for more. I wanted to feel loved. My life was characterized by a false perception of love and I was yearning to connect to someone who could truly love me. As I grew into my teenage years, I started to take God more seriously and began attending church, but the impact of my experiences followed me. It dictated the way that I thought, moved and made decisions. My choices were rooted in my trauma. Church gave me a sense of purpose. Getting involved in various ministries was a coping mechanism to help me block out my reality.

The truth is, regardless of how much I tried to mask my heart, I would find myself looking for love from men in hopes that someone would still want to be with me. I found myself engaging in sexual relationships as a means for fulfillment. It didn't even make sense to me but I was constantly looking to find true love. There was a longing to fill the emptiness in my soul and to find love that wouldn't hurt me, steal from me and destroy me.

I engaged in multiple relationships, and I was struggling. No one ever knew. I felt like two people in one: trying to be a church girl while fulfilling the lust of the flesh. I was constantly at war. I was angry. There was so much guilt and shame, fear and defeat. I couldn't open up and tell my story. No one would believe me if I told anyway.

Being introduced to church did help me to recognize that I was currently living a dilemma. I was at war within myself. I needed a saviour. I needed the Saviour! My past had created a monster in me. I was addicted to finding love and engaging in relationships that a child of God had no business being a part of.

In 2006, I had broken off an engagement with my boyfriend with every intention of staying single and "finding" myself. That did not last very long. Soon after, I found myself reconnecting with my previous boyfriend, who was one of my best friends. We decided on another attempt to be in a relationship. We had known each other for a very long time from going to church together and we became very close friends. We knew that we wanted to do things the "right" way, but we constantly found ourselves doing them the wrong thing.

We each had our own trials to face, but we were struggling through them together. We tried to help each other, keep each other accountable, and maintain the utmost level of integrity, but we failed every time. I knew I had issues, but instead of me truly seeking help to overcome my hurdles, I just masked them with the "love" I was receiving.

Eventually, enough was enough. God was ready for me to blossom. He was ready for me to let go of my inconsistencies, so he commanded and demanded I stop the games. He was tired of the hypocrisy—me singing His praises during the day and singing my partners praises during the night. I was tired of me playing house. I was tired of me living a life that was contrary to His will. He was tired of my hypocrisy; he was disgusted with my intentional inconsistency. God was ready to help me shift.

Broken but not destroyed

As I held a positive pregnancy test in my hands, I knew that my indiscretions would be exposed. I wasn't ready yet. I wasn't ready to become responsible for another human being. I was only 23! I was a youth leader, choir director, praise team singer and I had hit rock bottom. I went through a period of depression and shame. I tried to cover it up. I tried to stop the process in its tracks, but PLAN B did not work. Chastisement came from ALL angles. Disappointment set in among those whom I loved dearly. I had to step down from all positions. Those who once looked up to me, now looked down at me. This was the moment where my boyfriend and I could have run away, but we did not. We decided to get married. Was that the right thing to do? Our pastor said that it was the worst thing we could have done. He said getting married right away was not the answer.

Now that the whole church knew of our indiscretion; it was difficult to attend church without the fear of being ridiculed and scrutinized. Nevertheless, we kept on attending. We decided that it was time for the church to practise what it preached. Forgiveness was a central teaching, and if the church members considered themselves to be Christians, they would have to forgive us. We decided that it no longer mattered what people thought. We were indeed washed by the blood of the lamb.

We kept sitting in our marked seats, right in the front row. We kept singing our praises to God, because we knew we had been forgiven. We believed God and took him at His word. Not only did we continue to attend church, we continued to assist those who were leading because despite our struggles, we DID love God and wanted to serve him. It was during this time that God inspired me to write a song. A song that helped me through this low point in my life; a song that gave me life. It is entitled, "I Love You Forevermore". The chorus captures the essence of how God looks at us (his children).

He said, I love you forever more, my life I lay down,
I love you forever more, my blood is poured all over you.
You don't know the change he's made. I love you is what he said.

Even though my life wasn't perfect, I felt free. I felt free because now that I had hit rock bottom, there was nowhere to go but up. Jesus picked me up. He scooped me up in his arms and helped me through my circumstances. Standing strong during the battle was difficult, but God worked it all out for my good. As a result of our transparent situation, several young people came forward to me in confidence seeking guidance and direction. They felt comfortable enough to open up to me about some of their struggles and addictions. God used my situation for good; it was a testament of his power and saving grace. God was able to speak through me; using my personal situation to empower others.

Struggling Seedling

After the birth of our baby, my life did not get easier, but rather things became increasingly difficult. While I tried my best to push on and live strong, I faced many hurdles, many challenges and many defeats. Instead of dealing with my baggage and seeking to experience true healing, I kept putting a Band-Aid on my life. Even though I was now a mother and a wife, my suitcase was FULL of all the hurt and pain of my past childhood. It was filled with pain from selfish decisions made by my husband to fulfill his own desires without any regard for how it would impact me and our budding family. His choosing to fulfill the lusts of the flesh cost me a great deal, physically, emotionally and spiritually. Even though I forgave him, I still walked around wounded. Even so, God was still working. I was a work in progress. I STILL am a work in progress.

Despite the challenges faced within my marriage, we continued, and God began to open doors. He constantly reminded me that despite my childhood experiences that lacked love, despite the choices I made growing up into adulthood, he loved me and had great plans for me. He blessed my womb and gave me three more beautiful children. He provided for all of my needs according to his riches, and he began to work several miracles in my life that showed his unfailing, unconditional love for me.

I Believe in Miracles

Living in the city is not an easy task when raising children. Busy streets, dangerous neighbourhoods and a polluted environment were not conducive to raising children. At this point, I had just had my third child and was in a state of sadness. We did not live in a neighbourhood that was ideal for raising our children. I began to fast and pray to God to make a way for us to move into a house where we would have sufficient space and land to raise our children. I no longer wanted to be in the city, but I did not see a way out.

God moved in my life and brought an opportunity to my husband, enabling us to rent a house with the option to buy in upstate New York. When my husband told me about the opportunity, I could see it was God's hand as I was praying about it without my husband even knowing. We did not have all the t's crossed and the i's dotted, but we trusted God and moved upstate. It was the best decision we could have ever made, and I am so grateful that we did.

Living upstate was wonderful for our family. We got connected to the local YMCA; we joined the local Seventh-day Adventist church; and my two children were enrolled in school. The third baby was in daycare and I had a job. Life was good. God is good. I thought that I had everything figured out and my life was all set. However, God had different plans for me.

While my husband and I thought we were done having children, God surprised us with one more; I was pregnant. This was a tough pill to swallow, as we wondered how we could afford one more. As I journeyed through this pregnancy experience, God reminded me that I once had a desire to homeschool my children. While I had always wanted to do so, at this point in my life it didn't seem feasible. My husband did not have a stable job bringing in consistent income, but I did as an occupational therapist. I was the one bringing in the funds that supported our life. How would homeschooling make sense? I began to pray and fast and decided that I would have to trust God completely. If he made a way for me before, I knew that he would do it again.

It was May 2014. My baby would soon be delivered and I decided to let my job know that I would not be coming back to work after my child was born. It was scary because my husband still did not have a stable job. The moment I let my job know that I would not be coming back, my husband called me to let me know that he was hired as minister of music at a United Methodist church, as well as the music coordinator at the local YMCA. Two-part time jobs to make up the full-time salary we needed to live! Praise God! God made a way for me to stay home with my four children, so I could be the one to raise them and homeschool them. It was truly a blessing, as this was my heart's desire when I only had one child.

Living upstate in the house we first moved into was nice. It was spacious, had a huge backyard and there was an option for us to buy it. Things initially went well, but after living in the house for a year, things began to go wrong. The basement flooded, which caused damage in the basement. The owner blamed my family for causing this flood and demanded that we pay for repairs. We called the city to have them come in and inspect the home to determine the cause. It was determined that the flood was caused by a backed-up sewage pipe from the street and it was not our fault. Even so, we had to move. We ended up moving into a three-bedroom apartment since we were not yet in a position to buy a home. We lived in the apartment for a couple of years. This is the home where my fourth child was born, and it was the home where I began my homeschooling.

As our family grew and homeschooling took over the whole house, I knew it was time for us to move again. Moving was not an easy task for us as we had some credit issues. Without credit, you can hardly get anything. Moving was not going to be as simple as A-B-C. However, what is impossible with man is possible with God!

My husband and I committed to praying for increase, healing, strength, deliverance, wisdom, power, glory, forgiveness, protection and direction. We committed 30 days to a series of fasts and prayers. One of the things on the prayer list was a new place to move into. We didn't want just another apartment, but a house that we could eventually call our own. We prayed for one big enough for homeschooling and for us to live comfortably.

We decided that during the fast we would read a book called Draw the Circle: The 40 Day Prayer Challenge by Mark Batterson. This book was truly a blessing for us. On Day 7 the word from God said that it's not enough to say that we have faith; we have to ACT on that faith. This was a pivotal point for us because at that time we were to let the leasing office know whether or not we would be renewing our lease, which was set to expire. That reading moved us to not only trust God to provide a new home but we were going to act on that trust. That same day, I went down to the leasing office and put in our notice to vacate. Did I know where we would be moving? No. Did we have to move in 30 days? Yes. Would it be easy to find a place with our situation credit wise? No. This was purely a leap of faith and for the first time during this process I felt the peace of God surround me. Some called us foolish and said that our decision didn't make any sense. You see with God, 1+1 equals a multiplicity of answers. The answer never adds up and never makes sense.

On Day 18 of the fast we were scheduled to see a home. After seeing so many homes that weren't right or didn't work out, I was tired of my emotions going up and down. So, I prayed a specific prayer that morning. I said, "Dear

Lord, we are going to see another house today that can potentially be ours. Lord, I am asking for you to make it very clear whether or not this house is for us. If this house is for us, may I see a flock of ravens fly across the sky. If I don't see the birds, then I know that we must keep looking. Lord, I want this process to bring you glory."

That morning we saw the house. It was a huge house that was walking distance from the local YMCA where my husband worked. There was adequate space for a classroom, big bedrooms for the children and good living space. The house was perfect for us. After seeing the house, I went outside and looked up to the sky. There was not a bird in sight. My heart sank, but I was prepared to continue trusting God. The real estate agent was willing to put in an application for us, but I didn't get my hopes up. I didn't see those birds! After seeing the house, we continued on our way to attend our homeschool co-op.

That afternoon as we were heading back home, I happened to look up in the sky as the sun was setting. I was shocked to see a flock of ravens! I started praising God for answering my prayers and providing a house for us to move to. That house was meant to be ours! Once I got home, I received a call from the real estate agent, stating that the landlord wanted to meet my family for an interview! I called my husband and told him my prayer and how God had answered. He was also very happy. The interview was scheduled for the following Sunday and the real estate agent informed me that there was also another family interviewing for the house as well. I struggled with feelings of doubt, but kept pressing onward.

Sunday arrived and we were headed to the house to meet the homeowner. I was struggling and God knew this was on my heart and mind. As I was driving and about to turn the corner to the house, a flock of ravens flew right in front of my car! I praised God and thanked him for his reassurance that the house was ours. We met the homeowner and she asked us questions while looking at our documents. She seemed to be pleased but we still weren't sure. Two days later, we received the phone call that the home was ours! Once again, God had come through.

God has placed us in this neighbourhood as a beacon of light. Our influence in our town has become strong and we have become well known in our community. God also placed me in this environment because he had a plan for my life to cross paths with some key individuals who would actually help me on my journey towards true healing. I have made some great acquaintances, but God blessed me with two other sisters in addition to my blood sister, who also moved and joined me in the Middletown community.

When we first met my dear friend, we had no idea what God had in store for us. Now that we are four years in, I see why God allowed us to meet. God has used my friends as well as my sister to help me realize I am still bruised and broken. The multiple violations stole my happiness and instead of me dealing with it head on, I chickened out and put another Band-Aid on top of the wound. I realize now, it is time for me to face my fears. It is time for me to look at my past dead in the eye and kill it. It is time to release the chains that have me bound.

Looking Up

I cannot say that I have truly healed, because that would be lying. I am still broken, but for the first time I have found my way. In order to experience true healing, you have to face the reality of your problem. Look at it straight in the eye. Call it what it is — a thorn in your side. Accept it for what it is. The next step is to be transparent. So often, I would find myself covering things up or downplaying my feelings and not realizing that I was digging myself into a deeper hole. The key is to face your issue and talk about it.

I am so grateful for Sis Arias United, created by my sister Contessa and me, since it gives me the platform to become more transparent with my feelings. Sis Arias United represents two sisters coming together, using our stories to empower, motivate and uplift others to push through the many obstacles that tend to befall us on life's journey. Once again, transparency is a prerequisite for healing. Once you remove your thorn and become transparent, you will be well on your way to healing. I am still on my journey to true healing.

As I continue on my road of healing, I must remember that we are becoming who God created us to be. Life's journey constantly chisels away at us, moulding and refining us to the place where we can be free to spread our wings and soar. You WILL have your opportunity to spread your wings and fly! Keep pressing, don't give up, and seize the opportunity when it comes because it is coming sooner than you think. As we continue to press on through our individual journeys, we have to remember that love is the answer. Love God, love yourself and love others.

LITTLE BLACK GIRL

Where is that little black girl that I used to know?
Round and stout with the kinkiest black afro

Where is that little black girl that I used to see?
Playing freely with her toys and her favourite Barbie

Where is that little black girl who used to laugh so loud?
Her laugh so contagious, it would immediately ignite a crowd

Where is that little black girl whose imagination was so free?
She would write about anything, you just let her be

Where is that little black girl who always used to smile?
A grin so wide, ear to ear, something she could not hide

A little black girl robbed by life's woes
Innocence snatched by ravenous folks
Her smile, her glee, her freedom slipped away
Traded with sadness, and sorrow and overwhelming dismay

That little black girl should be looking ahead
for all the joys that life SHOULD bring
Instead she looks back at the freedom of her past,
hoping that song she could once more sing

WHO AM I?

I am!

*Little black girl, little black girl
You've experienced what we call life
This road is not easy, it's filled with undue strife*

*So realize in your pity,
that you have to rise above*

*Look to the stars,
reach for the clouds whose end is way up above*

*Yes, you've had setbacks,
yes, life is hard*

*Yes, you live with the weight of your past,
bearing the biggest, ugliest, nastiest scar*

Raise the bar!

*In the midst of your weight and constant state of doom,
tap into your inner greatness and let all your thoughts of greatness consume you*

*Arise out of this state of despair,
you have little ones following behind you, so please beware*

*Their success has some stance on the choices YOU make,
so don't hesitate to be great!*

*Little black girl . . . find your smile
Little black girl . . . find your joy*

*Little black girl, you were destined to be the greatest you,
Stand tall and believe*

CHAPTER 8

I Choose To Love

I AM Yolanda Desouza

> *"Jesus doesn't love me this I know,*
> *for the Bible tells me so . . . no Jesus loves me?*
> *No Jesus loves me."*

As I sang this hymn to myself, I wrote down the names of all the members of my family who didn't love me, from aunts to uncles to cousins. I wanted to die of a despicable disease. Perhaps cancer. No, AIDS. I wanted them all to suffer for ignoring me and making me feel as if I didn't exist.

For as long as I could remember, I had felt unloved, disconnected and unworthy of love. There was this nagging and persistent ache in my heart, combined with an overwhelming feeling that I was not good enough. I felt alone, not because of anything anyone ever did, but it was as though a part of me was missing. From an early age, I also felt that I was angry with the world. I felt unstable, unsettled, as if I never really belonged. You could say that I had my fair share of love lessons to learn in life.

My earliest memory brings me back to Bridlewood Mall. I was three years old and nestled in between my granny and grandpa. I was leaning on my grandpa and looking at the people passing by, and out of the corner of my eye, I glimpsed my mom and dad walking past us, hand in hand. My smile disappeared and my eyes welled up with tears. Why weren't they noticing me? Why did dad have his arm around mom? Were they trying to get rid of me? They had forgotten me, I was sure.

I started to choke up and cry. They both turned around and my mom walked over and said, "Yolanda, what's wrong baby?" They came over to console a young girl whose inconsolable cry filled her with anger and emptiness. I was getting crankier by the minute. I didn't like seeing my parents' public display of affection. It would take decades for me to see that I was jealous.

I Choose to Die

By six years old, I believed I was unlovable. I spent most of my days alone, watching television in our basement. "I hope I develop AIDS," I told myself as I daydreamed on the sofa or stared out my window at the evening sky.

One day, my sister was working on schoolwork at our kitchen table, with '80s alternative music playing in the background. She was eight years older than me and had a unique friendship with mom that I couldn't compete with. That day, I found myself vying for her attention, fiddling with her papers, or sitting blankly at the table alone.

"Go away," my sister uttered with annoyance. I turned to my mom to fill my void.

"Mom, what are you making?" I asked.

"Pilaf. Dinner should be ready soon; go watch some TV." Mom didn't even raise her head from what she was doing.

I sauntered away and sat alone at the table in the family room. I wrote a goodbye note.

I want to die of AIDS. I don't want to live. No one loves me. Not Richard, Clive, Jeremy, Michelle, Debbie, Derek, Lucas, Sarita, Annie, Tony, Alda and Pete. They all don't like me, including mom and dad.

I felt deserted. Tears streaked down my cheeks, and my forehead ached with pain. Though I wanted to sob from the depths of my bowels, I held it in and tore the note into pieces and threw it in the garbage. I ran upstairs and locked myself in my favourite spot, the bathroom. I looked into the mirror and watched myself cry and felt sorry for myself. I wanted to punish those people who hurt me.

They ignored me, and I wanted to make them hurt as much as me. I huddled on the floor, and let all the agony and disappointment just run its course.

As I lay there crying, I heard a voice. "I know what you wrote."

A feeling of sheer terror coursed through me as I looked up and saw the torn up fragments of paper in my sister's hands.

"I'm going to tell mom and dad," she said. I panicked. I was paralyzed by fear that my secret was out, and I had to think fast, out of sheer embarrassment.

"I'm joking!" I blatantly lied. "I was bored and made up the whole thing!" I ran off to my room and my feet felt like they were giving way beneath me. I curled up in my bed and replayed my story of self-pity in my head. I told myself that if I died, they would experience great sadness. They would regret not paying attention to me. I replayed this in my mind so many times that pretty soon, playing the victim became my identity.

I Choose Dad

"What a beautiful day, oh what a beautiful day. What a beautiful day for Sharon, Yolanda, mommy and daddy."

Oh, how I looked forward to those Saturday mornings

where I'd hear my dad sing those songs to us as he pulled opened the blinds to let in the morning light. It made me feel like I was part of something and belonged to a family!

My father was very important to me. More than anyone, he validated my existence. He took joy and pleasure in who I was. He was always happy around me, and I got a lot of attention. Seeing his blue Marquis pulling up to the driveway after an afternoon shift was the most wonderful sight. He would sometimes be carrying a treat like Reese's Pieces, Sour Keys or pizza, and my sister and I would rush to the door to get our special treat.

He was a blue collar factory worker by day, and a musician by night. He was popular; everyone liked him. Because of his work he was rarely at home. When my dad was home, I'd occupy myself with television while he slept after his long shifts. My parents would spend a lot of time together taking naps, and they seemed to have a better relationship with each other than they did with me or my sister. I longed for the time I would spend with my father.

My sister was usually on the telephone or listening to her "ghetto blaster." My mom often spent time with my sister, since she was older and focused on her studies. I felt they had a bond and had more things in common than I did with either of them. Looking back, I felt like an outsider. I didn't see how I belonged. The only person I connected to was either away, doing shift work, or playing in a band. I felt like my dad's pet, just waiting for him to come home. In fact, my sister would always say I was dad's favourite. Pretty soon, I chose to identify with my dad because he gave me a lot of attention and looked happy when I was around, which is what I so desperately wanted.

I Choose Fear

My sensitivities and attachments made moving from my childhood home extremely difficult. Leaving Scarborough was a pivotal moment in my life. Saying goodbye to school friends on the last day of school wasn't easy. My teacher got the Grade 2 class to write goodbye letters to me. I felt special and honoured, until I read Kevin's. Kevin was a boy whom I liked, and who I thought might have liked me. He was quiet and withdrawn like me, and I thought we had a connection. Kevin's letter said, "Hope you have a nice Christmas, but a horrible stay at your new school, and hope you get measles and a sickness and die."

I felt so distraught that even now as I write this, it is hard to remember all of the positive outpouring of love I received from the rest of the class. I was panicked and paralyzed with fear. I wondered how Kevin was able to reflect back to me the exact same feelings I had about myself. The impact of his letter would go on for years. His view of me reinforced how I felt about myself.

Shortly after that day, we moved into our new home and I began going to a new school. I took the bus to and from school, and I recall one incident on the bus that stayed with me for many years.

It was a frosty, snowy day, and I wanted to stay home for some reason. I had this uneasy feeling in my tummy that was making me into a bundle of nerves. I wanted to curl up on my couch and be safe. Despite this, I went to school as usual.

The school bus arrived that afternoon to take us home and the kids were hollering, as they always did as we waited for the bus. I ignored them and waited patiently, keeping my fingers warm inside my coat pockets. I nuzzled myself inside my hood and made myself invisible to the busy noise of hate, swearing and boys muscling each other into the snow.

Our bus arrived and somehow I ended up getting on the bus first and looked for a place to sit with my new friend, Nadine. The rest of the kids shoved in, and hurriedly tried to make their way to the back of the bus. I heard bellowing, catcalls and jokes. The boys were still wired from their snow fight and to try and ignore them I pressed my head against the frosty window frame. I felt the rattling of the bus as its engine began to gain speed to take us home.

I began daydreaming about love, and fantasized having a big circle of friends, and what it will be like when I'm older. I envisioned myself anywhere but there. One of the boys, a rambunctious one, started telling jokes and interrupted my concentration with his croaky voice. I pressed my head closer to the window, ignoring his howling sounds. I immediately wanted to be invisible. I heard the boy's voice getting louder, and his laughter became sinister. I knew that the tension in the air on that bus could be cut with a knife.

Then I heard it. "Hey, 'Paki' girl," he called out. It rang out so loud that I was shocked. I became frozen with fear; I was silent. He couldn't be talking to me, could he? He continued to call that name, and at this point the bus became frantic with laughter. I continued to sink lower and lower. He proceeded to gawk at me, and then scooted over to the empty seat beside me to get my attention. He yanked on my jacket, and talked into my face. The heat under my brow grew, and the students became silent. I knew something very bad was about to happen, and that is when the bus hit a speed bump. The kids on the bus jumped, and the boy took that opportunity to jump right onto my lap and let out the largest and loudest fart. The kids began to laugh hysterically. I felt like I was an animal caged up in a zoo; I was there for their entertainment!

Mortified, I pretended I didn't notice, wishing I could erase this memory from my mind. I left that bus sobbing, panicked and alone. I carried myself through the front door to my house, raced up the flight of stairs, collapsed underneath my thick bed covers and mourned myself to sleep. "Again, another male who hates me," I wept. "Another name to add to the growing list of people who don't like me." As this list grew, so did my own self victimization. I felt worthless, not good enough.

As I continued to grow up in white, suburban Mississauga, I was nerdy and silenced by my shyness. I was bullied and had very few friends. I was chosen last for school teams and dances. I was ignored and ostracized by the rest of the white girls in my class. Unacceptance was the predominant feeling of my life at that time. Being bullied affected me more than I thought, and had severe consequences not only on my personality but on my feelings of self-worth. I was drowning in self-pity, and this feeling stayed with me throughout elementary and high school, and right into adulthood.

I Choose Brokenness

"Sit up straight. Fix your hair. Dress prettier."

So much attention was put on the way I looked that any form of intelligence I might have had just disappeared. My looks began to change, and the emphasis was on how to improve my looks rather than my faltering self-esteem. I was left feeling that there was something wrong with me; boys never asked me to dance, and I was awkward and lanky with wacky hair. It wasn't until Grade 8 that my looks began to transform.

My parents put me in a Barbizon modelling school, and I began to feel pretty and receive attention from boys. I was hanging out with older girls from Barbizon and getting fake IDs to go to the clubs. I slowly but surely began to come alive! My body was pretty curvaceous and I didn't look like a typical 13 year old. The attention I began getting from boys replaced my attachment towards my family.

As I grew older I began to find countless broken and abusive relationships with men who would use me for their own sexual gratification. I searched countlessly for men who paid any type of attention to me. I recall feeling completely depressed and utterly heartbroken if a guy never returned a phone call after a date, or broke up with me a few months later. My fears of abandonment and not being loved were still very much alive. I was so fragile.

When I did find a good man, I would sabotage the relationship. My pattern of rejecting good men continued because I didn't feel worthy of "good" love. I wasn't used to this type of love — it felt foreign to my body, like a virus — and so I rejected it and I rejected them. Instead, the men I would identify with were merely mirrors of me. They were boys who never grew up or had grown up alone and feeling unloved, only to become adults who didn't know how to have healthy relationships. You see, we are given only as much as we think we deserve. I felt I was nothing and I was incapable of receiving the "good love," so this is what I got.

My teens and twenties consisted of worrying, dramatization and ruminating on every failed relationship. I would talk on the phone for countless hours about the heartache and pain of what other people did to me. I felt alone and betrayed, similar to the pain and situations I encountered as a young girl. My point here is that these feelings never go away. They only become replaced with different situations, themes and faces. All these feelings are tied in with low self-worth and mental illness. We think that at some point we will get it together and that our dysfunction will go away, but it doesn't.

I mistook glimpses and shreds of attention for love. Men didn't have to do much except buy me something nice and take me out for expensive dinners. I didn't know what love and respect felt like because I had none. I jumped from relationship to relationship with men who were married, men who had girlfriends and men who cheated on me. I used this attention to fill the deep-seated void — the void that could be filled by my parents.

I Choose to Heal

I became a corrections officer when I was 21 years old. That is where I began to really experience the grief of life. I had forgotten about my inner sadness because I was preoccupied for eight years with "distractions" and "avoidance," with intoxicants and teenage drama. I didn't know who the real Yolanda was; I somehow lost her along the way. Because of this, I ended up in an abusive relationship with a co-worker who emotionally and psychologically abused me. To put things into perspective, I was in a relationship with a man who also had a long-term girlfriend. I still allowed myself to enter into a relationship with him because it gave me more attention than I'd get from being alone. I had his attention, daily phone calls, and physical contact. I didn't know what self-respect was, because I didn't grow up knowing myself.

Eventually, when the courageous side of me kicked in, I tried to break things off. He began to stalk me, and towards the very end of the relationship he used physical force to gain power and control over me. He was taking out his insecurity by getting angry and putting me down. He would constantly play with my emotions and use mind games to control me. I allowed myself to be in this toxic relationship all for the sake of what I thought was love.

Thankfully, while going through this breakup, I found a safety net of friends who were around to comfort me despite my "inconsolable" cries. I found solace in my new friendship circle; my old teenage friends were now replaced with new adulthood friends!

I began to try to turn things around in my life. I attended numerous self-esteem, anger-management and conflict-resolution groups. However, nothing was working for me and I began questioning myself. Why wasn't this helping me? The answer was because I was NOT taking responsibility for MY LIFE. I always wanted OTHER people to do it for me. I would rely on therapy groups, counsellors, friends and other people to dictate what was good. I was self-centered and only thought of myself and how I could take, take, take from others by unloading my garbage onto them.

Looking back, I think that this phase of my twenties was my cocoon phase because I got outside help and attended numerous workshops on self-esteem. However, these were Band-Aid solutions that got me through the lows of my life. They were bricks being set up for the bigger, catastrophic events that would later shake my adult years. My therapy was preparing me to embrace a spiritual awakening, leaving me with foundations of learned behaviours I could use during this process. It was in my 30s when the magic finally began, and the work of true catharsis took place.

I Choose Pain

My therapy was moving in a positive direction, and I was working at a job that I loved. I had no idea that this was when I was about to be shaken to my core.

"Hark, is it you?!" I asked in amazement. I dashed into the arms of a man who I hadn't seen in 10 years. I felt a surge of electricity course through my body. We jumped into each other's embrace as if no time had gone by. We had known each other since Grade 9 and he had moved to the States. Now, we were reunited once again.

We found ourselves head over heels in love, and spent day and night making up for lost time. He had just got out of prison, and within two weeks of him being out we had started our relationship. Now, you'd think that from all the therapy I'd had, the self-help books I'd read and the volatile relationships I had endured, that my self-esteem would kick in and say "NO." Unfortunately, I was desperate once again for love. We "fell in love" within three weeks. I knew he was vulnerable, and I was too, but once again it felt good to be loved. It felt good to be with someone who wanted to be with me and make long-term plans. So, I fell head over heels, forgot all that I learned, my thick shell came down and I allowed myself to feel vulnerable and safe. I felt as if he had every part of my heart. I felt that he and I would be together forever; we made plans for marriage, and kids, and spent all of our time together. I thought I had found true happiness, and that my constant childhood daydreaming of relationships and love would finally end. My dreams were being met and my old hurts and pains subsided. It was blissful, until the honeymoon phase ended and reality set in. Boy, was I about to learn a lesson in life!

After a few months, Hark became reaccustomed with life on the outside and started doing as he liked. He distanced himself from me and my inner demons came screaming out with a vengeance. I became needy and was constantly asking questions. Where are you going? Why didn't you invite me? Don't you love me? Why is your sister texting you so much? I would cry and sob. I didn't like that I wasn't at the center of his world. In fact, the more I felt he was slipping away from me, the tighter I held on.

"Yolanda, you are needy. I can't take this," he said. What? I am needy? How was I needy? I cried when my needs weren't met, and I thought that was what people did when they felt the way I was feeling.

"Stop behaving like a child. I need a woman. Where is that secure woman I fell in love with? You make me feel like I'm walking on eggshells. Nothing is ever good enough for you, and you are impossible to please!" he told me.

My *heart sank*. My chance at love was slipping through my fingers. I was six years old again, and my inner child had come out to sabotage me. My self-fulfilling prophecy was coming true. "No one loves me, this I know . . ." I said to myself. My final moments of happiness were slipping away. I stared at him blankly as he continued to scold me. I was an empty chalice and wanted him to fill me up. The relationship eventually ended after six months, and so did my life.

I Choose to Seek and Find

The God of the Universe gives us our ultimate wake-up

call. When we are ready to face the music, we are thrown into real despair. My relationship ended and I died on the inside. Just three months later, I had lost all of my creativity. My menstruation stopped, along with my ability to conceive. I was told that I didn't have 10 years to wait to have a child. I was told that at the age of 31, my body would start to behave like a 50-year-old's. This was too much to handle for a woman who'd placed her whole purpose on finding the perfect partner, being a mother and having a family. Who'd want an infertile woman?

I couldn't believe that this was happening to me, on top of the other disorders I'd faced. Countless doctors, fertility clinics, and endocrine and other kinds of specialists all delivered the same bad news. I was totally and completely devastated.

Once again, the ground beneath me was ripped away and I was back in that dark place. I was alone again, like when I was four years old and watching television in my basement. I couldn't even muster the strength to phone my therapist because panic had gripped my heart. I felt as if I was in a hurricane and it had torn me to pieces.

My future was bleak and I needed to be healed. I couldn't understand it, but this was my identity now. This event is what spearheaded the actual change, dictating who I would become. It would start to challenge all my old notions, friendships, the men I used to date and my false beliefs.

This started a process of endless searching. The next eight years would be a journey of finding myself through various cults, religions, spiritual paths, healings and herbal medicine. I started spending thousands of dollars on every healer who would promise to help me. After spending so much money, it ultimately was up to me to wake up to the truth. No one could do it for me. I had to do it alone. Eventually I became a new Yolanda, and the old one died.

I Choose to Let Go

I came to depend on God and my angels for guidance and love. I knew there was power in the faith of God. I knew that I had to do the work myself in order to transcend my circumstances. This is when I came to the understanding that through my tears and sorrow I was releasing old baggage.

At this time, I also came across a book called *A Course in Miracles,* which emphasizes the need to look within, and to give our emotions to Christ. Christ holds our emotions for us temporarily, while we do the work. For the first time, I learned the power of FORGIVENESS. I learned that the unsettling feelings of my past, which had haunted me for so long, came to me through my relationships with others. At this time, I revisited the failed relationships, and my anger with the men who left me and abandoned me. I had viewed every man in my life as a cheater, as someone who had issues and lacked self-respect. I had not seen these relationships as teachers or as reflections of who I was. My perception of my father and what I viewed as abandonment is what I needed to acknowledge. My perception of people made me angry and apathetic towards them. I knew I needed to start forgiving and working on all the relationships in my life.

I started to keep a forgiveness journal and wrote daily about anyone I carried ill feelings towards. Regardless of how big or small I perceived an incident to be, I would write it in my journal and as I closed the journal each night, I would make a conscious decision to stop reliving the story.

Forgiveness has been the hardest part in overcoming darkness, and continues to be a struggle today. If I am attached to an old memory, caused by a person who triggered me, it can be difficult for me to let it go. Despite my struggles with forgiveness, I have learned to forgive. I have forgiven the class that bullied me, because they taught me to look within to see the fear that paralyzed me. I prayed for peace of mind, heart and words. I asked to change the anxiety from fear to love. Once I started to direct love and kindness towards my old tormentors, my perception was altered. I came to see that when I embraced their level of anger and hatred, I became those exact qualities. Love and kindness don't equate to condoning or ignoring. It's simply speaking your truth in all situations without worry, stress and the attachment to your emotions. I learned to ask Christ for guidance and this was the first time in my life that I had learned not to give my "problems" and "feelings" much attention. I had to face darkness in order to release it, otherwise I would never know that it existed within. I learned from my endless soul searching to go to God through the medium of prayer and forgiveness.

I now classify myself as "free." I am tied to God through faith, but not through any organized religion or spiritual practice. I now honour all of my emotions and accept all the mistakes within me because they are part of human existence. Freedom means not getting bogged down by the smallness and pettiness of life, or obsessing over our faults. We live in a human body, and when annoyance, disturbance or frustration creep in, we must become aware of them and send them to the light. Be thankful for this emotion arising in you so you can become aware of it and surrender it.

We live a long life and pretending that negative emotions won't get hold of us sometimes is living in denial. We should honour all our truths, so that those emotions won't have a lasting effect on our lives. It is easy to think that the shadow of anger and sadness are life sentences. I see now that it's a temporary state — these emotions rise and pass. It's the story we attach to the sensations of anger and sadness that have debilitating effects.

Throughout much of my life, I was mad at God, but this was because I couldn't hear him through my own sadness and anger. He was talking to me all along through a helper or a friend guiding me onto the right path. God's messages weren't coming in the way I wanted or expected. So I got mad when he wasn't answering me. I wasn't speaking God's language of love; instead I was talking through fear, hurt and disempowerment. As I began to clear away these emotions, I came to see that God is felt through the stillness and quietness of our hearts, and not in the distractions our ego sets up for us.

Today, I don't dwell on my shadows. The more I continue on this journey, the less these shadows have an impact on my life. This has been the most liberating step to becoming myself. All I have ever wanted was LOVE. I learned that to search for love is useless, because we create and find this love within ourselves first. This love is always within; we just need to drown out the outside world, and quiet our inner critic in order to feel the love within us. It is within ALL of us. We only need to tap into that energy potential and sit quiet in the midst of the storm in order to connect with our beloved creator — God of the Universe.

Jesus loves me this I know, for the Bible tells me so. Little ones who cry out loud, they are weak but he is strong. Yes, Jesus loves me. Yes, Jesus loves me, for the Bible tells me so.

CHAPTER 9

High Up, Fallen, Back Up

I AM Tatiana Lopez

Sofía screamed and cried. She was standing with her feet on the ground, holding herself up against the living room wall in her house, as her knees gave out little by little. What she had sworn sacredly to uphold before God was broken: her marriage.

A few hours earlier, she had found a business card on Marco's desk from a store called X-Treme.

"What is this?" Sofia asked. She masked her anxiety and sadness with a curious tone. Even as she spoke, she wondered if her red eyes and heavy breathing revealed her true feelings. Marco was speechless, and several moments of silence passed before he finally responded.

"I am in love with another woman," he announced. "I am going to be with her." His words hit Sophia in the chest like a baseball bat.

"Why? WHY?" Sofia demanded.

"You never appreciated me. She does," he responded. She would remember later the other words spoken by Marco before he left: "It's your fault!" Marco left. He left with nothing but the clothes on his back. As her world collapsed, Sofia stood there looking at the business card that ended her marriage. The house suddenly felt very cold to her. "Why?!?!" she screamed as she sunk to the floor.

The Divine Revelation

Desperate for fresh air and clarity, Sofia left her house. "A walk will do me some good," she whispered to herself. As she walked by San Pedro Church, something in her heart told her to go inside. The priest's voice drew her back to present. She sat down and joined the mass. Among the murmur of praying parishioners, Sofia began a heartfelt spiritual plea. "My God, please help me. Something has gone horribly wrong," she whispered. "Please restore my marriage." A bone-chilling feeling ran through her body. She felt as though it was a warning, meant to prepare her for something extremely difficult. Immediately, the words of the priest hit her ears:

"The Lord of Heaven and Earth will restore you."

Sofia left the church and walked across the street, stunned by what she had just experienced. Walking along she saw an outlet mall and there was a voice inside that told her she must go inside. She walked in the door of the mall, looking around. Without any rational explanation, she felt magnetically drawn to the third floor. She felt perplexed until her eyes landed on one specific store, with a sign reading X-Treme. She had seen this name various times on her and her husband's bank statements. She assumed it was a sports apparel store, as her husband loved to hike.

It soon became clear it was not a sports apparel store. Hundreds of sex toys lined the shelves of the store. She had never stepped foot in a place like this before. Her mind was on overdrive. "What about me?" she thought, eyes bulging as she walked through the store. "What about me? What am I in his life? I gave him my heart, my life, my dreams, and now it's all thrown in the garbage." The sting of betrayal, like a knife, was plunged into her chest. In that moment, the light in her soul dimmed. Darkness entered.

Sweet Encounters

For months, Marco had been leaving regularly for sexual encounters with his mistress, Milena. There were many times that Sofia could sense that something was different about her husband, but she could never put her finger on it. His demeanour was changing towards her, and she was often left wondering what happened to her loving husband. They were slowly drifting apart.

During one of Marco's secret encounters with Milena, Sofia had a car accident. She was shaken up and immediately called Marco for support. Little did she know he was lying between the sheets, making intense love with his mistress. Her phone call interrupted the moment.

"What is it, Sofia? I'm busy," Marco answered the phone abruptly.

Sofia was stunned by this, but she began to explain what had happened. "Sweetheart, I had a car accident. I need your help," she said.

Marco was furious. He was furious that such a magical moment with Milena was interrupted, and he was furious to have to deal with such a situation. He knew that the relationship he had with Sofia had to come to an end. It was blatantly obvious to him that any love he had for Sofia was gone. Frustrated, he left Milena to go help Sofia.

Marco arrived at the scene of the accident, which was not serious. Sofia had hit a car that was parked very close to her and damaged both cars. "Is this all you know how to do? Be reckless?" Marco said curtly. Sofia got into his car and felt nothing but shame. With tears in her eyes, she felt powerless to question why he was treating her that way. She just wanted to be with him in her moment of need, but he was cold and distant.

As they drove, Sofia thought to herself, "How can I be so in love with this man who rejects me constantly?" In her head she answered her question, "It's because you can't live without him." She tortured herself with more questions: "Why is he so cold towards me? Why won't he kiss me or hug me anymore? What happened to us?" It wounded her when Marco got mad instead of supporting her. She found herself wishing the Marco she knew would come back. The one who was there for her in the difficult times, with all the support in the world. "Where is MY Marco?" she wondered.

As soon as they got back to the house, Marco locked himself in his office. There he hid and chatted to his lover until late in the night. They talked about sexual desires and what they would do when they were together again, while Marco watched porn. Sofia, totally unaware of what was going on in his office, read a book and watched a movie. She fell asleep waiting for him to come to bed.

In the middle of the night, she touched his side of the bed looking to hug him, but he was nowhere to be found. She woke up worried and went to look for him. She knocked on his office door, which he recently began keeping locked.

"Marco are you going to come to sleep? What's going on?" Sofia said through the door.

"I will be there in a minute," Marco replied.

Sofia went back to bed, and a little while later Marco entered the room. He changed his clothes, lay down and turned away from her without saying anything. Not even good night. He closed his eyes and went to sleep. He was as cold as ice towards her. His heart and mind were elsewhere.

Sofia's Bubble

If anyone had a beautiful childhood, that person was Sofia. Her parents loved her very much and her life was full of privilege. She lived in a bubble of safety and protection, with endless opportunities. Unlimited hugs from her parents, delicious and nutritious food, playing with toys and games, and trips with her brothers and sisters around Costa Rica.

Her mother was dedicated, picking out cute outfits for her daughters and doing their hair daily. Her father worked very hard so that her mother could stay at home and care for the children. Sofia's mother loved animals. Their family had many pets, including bunnies, parrots and dogs. They lived in a beautiful little house, with a nice backyard where they played with their pets. She experienced never-ending laughter and smiles day to day. Overall, it was simply the ideal childhood.

When Sofia began to attend school, she immediately fell in love with learning. She had a grand imagination and was loved by her teachers. She loved to spend her time reading and growing her young mind. This love of learning continued on into high school. Her classmates thought she was a nerd, but she didn't care. It was during this time in high school that Sofia began to experience the harsh realities of life for the first time.

One day there was a staff meeting, and the students were left alone in the classroom. One group of students, with a reputation for bad behaviour, locked the doors and began to act like animals. They were taking off their shoes and jumping from desk to desk. Sofia was sitting quietly at her desk, trying to decide what she should be studying. The group of boys came over to her.

"Please, leave me alone. Don't touch me!" Sofia exclaimed.

"One, two, three!" the boys yelled in chorus, and pulled her out of her desk by force, tipping it over. They carried her over to a garbage can and dropped her inside. She was crying uncontrollably as everyone looked at her. No one came to help her and just watched while she pulled herself up on the rim of the garbage can.

On this day, her glass bubble began to crack. She realized that there were many things she did not know about reality.

Like a princess in a castle, she received a lot of protection and care, but outside the castle walls she had no idea how to defend herself.

The bullying continued from time to time and the only thing that helped was her passion for learning. She would try her best to focus on her schoolwork and not let the mistreatment get to her. Life was showing her that everything isn't always happy and perfect, but she wanted nothing to do with that reality. She just buried her head in her studies, desperately trying to keep her bubble intact.

The Soul Reincarnated

Barely a month had passed since Marco had left, and Sofia's glass bubble had finally broken. She experienced what she would later call a "psychotic madness." She could not sleep and she cried inconsolably. She could barely eat. Her soul bled for the loss of the love of her life.

"My love, why did you leave me? I loved you with the deepest part of my heart, with everything that I am and everything that I have," Sofia said over and over again. "What does she have that I don't?" She would cry towards heaven and beg God to do something to help her recover her love.

Sofia called Marco many times, trying to convince him to go to therapy. He denied her every time. He was already living with Milena and enjoying his new life. He was moving on with his life while Sofia was engulfed in pain. She rotated among melancholy, impotence and anger. She was driving herself crazy, asking a thousand times, "WHY?" She thought back on the happy memories they shared together and grieved heavily. Despite where they were today, they had once been happy.

Shortly after they were married, Sofia and Marco had travelled the entire country together, exploring many national parks and sharing memorable moments with different family members. They grew together intellectually and participated in a group of young future leaders in the country. The adventurous spirit of Marco captivated Sofia's heart. She respected his intelligence and analytical skills, and the social life they built together was perfect in her eyes.

In a rural area, they had bought a lot of land and filled it with many fruit trees. They sowed the seeds together. With care, their seeds germinated and became a beautiful forest. When the trees bore fruits, they picked them one by one, and happily shared them with their families. They planted together, watched it grow and ate together. Oh, how she longed to experience this again.

Healing Prayers

Sofia began to suffer from a growing depression. She

decided to visit a therapist, in hopes that she could pull herself out of her pit of despair.

"Doctor, it hurts so much. How could he abandon me? Please help me. The pain is stronger than I am," Sofia cried to her therapist, with swollen eyes. "I can't go on with this anxiety. It is killing my soul. I can't just sit here and do nothing. I have to do something. I have to go find Marco because I can't live without him. I don't want this reality!" Sofia cried.

"You must live your life one day at a time. Feel the pain of loss. It is over. He is gone. That is the reality," her therapist told her repeatedly, looking firmly in her eyes. She was insistent that this was reality, and Sofia must accept it.

Sofia tried to take her therapist's suggestions. She worked on supporting herself, ate a little, and continued going to her appointments. She also began visiting spiritual counsellors.

She went to see a spiritual counsellor named Patricia in the town of Heredia. During one of her visits, the counsellor called on the Holy Spirit while Sofia wept. Intense and fervent prayer flooded the atmosphere.

"God, help me please. I can't go on. Heal me. I want to be with you. Today and forever. You are my light and my salvation. You are my guide," Sofia called out. She felt her hands begin to burn, as if something very hot was touching them. She then felt a sense of peace envelope her, as a mother would lovingly wrap her baby in a blanket. Love inundated her soul, and the healing began to flourish. She cried harder than ever before, but this time it was tears of happiness.

"What is this?" Sofia asked Patricia.

"It is the Holy Spirit touching you. This is the beginning of your new life. Glory to God!" Patricia replied with a smile.

This spiritual force entered every part of her body, heart and soul. It was a moment she will never forget. From that moment on, when Sofia would pray, her hands would become very hot and she knew it was a sign that the Holy Spirit was present. It reminded her that He is always with her, cares for her and strengthens her. She continued to pray every day, and slowly she began to heal.

Finally the day came when Sofia was ready to move out of her parents' house and go back to the home she once shared with Marco. "Mom, Dad, I am going home. I need to start my life again. I need to go on," Sofia said. She hugged her parents and gratefully thanked them for their support during this difficult time. She thanked them for their constant encouragement, which had helped her heal. She thanked them from the bottom of her heart.

"You don't have to thank us," Sofia's father said. "We love you and we are always here to support you. Go start your new life." With one last hug, she got in her car and was on her way.

The Return

Since the night that Marco had left, that door to her home had not been opened. On her way to the house, Sofia picked up her friend, Laura. As they drove, Sofia turned to Laura and said, "I feel so alone. I don't know what I will do. However, I have faith and I must continue."

"You are a young, beautiful, professional woman with values. You will come out in front by the grace of God," Laura assured Sofia.

When they arrived at her home, Sofia paused for a moment, took a deep breath and went inside. Everywhere she looked there were memories of her life with Marco. Suddenly she felt weary of coming back to this place. Laura, sensing Sofia's struggle, tried to reassure her. "Don't worry, Sofia," she said. "Together we can make this home totally new."

Sofia felt a surge of hope. "Yes Laura! A new place to live. A new life!" she said, smiling back.

Together Laura and Sofia redecorated the entire house. They made it more feminine; it was a new space with a new style. They took down all the old photos and put flowers in their place. Little by little all the things from her old life disappeared, and new air flowed in.

As the days passed, Sofia found another motivating force bubbling up from within. She asked herself: what can

I do now that I had not done before? "I want to get an international master's degree!" she decided. Not long after, a well-known Spanish university admitted her, and she began to study hard. Communication and digital marketing began to occupy her mind. She started to grow in her knowledge and skills within the field. She spent many nights studying in her small office with soft music playing in an atmosphere of peace. Her dogs were always there to keep her company.

With a master's degree in hand, Sofia returned to her work. She wanted to venture out with new professional challenges. Not a year had gone by when there was an opportunity, an opening for an international position in a recognized Latin American organization. It was an amazing position, which included travelling to several countries.

The support her family gave her was crucial for her to be able to continue moving forward. Also, her continuous prayer for inner healing lifted her up more and more. Her face began to light up and her heart recovered little by little. Her parents and brother-in-law were key to her recovery, and she will forever be grateful to them.

One peaceful afternoon, Sofia wrote in her diary:

I no longer feel the need to beg for love. I have learned how to live alone, independently and maturely. I now have more connection with my family and my spiritual life. I have peace and hope, now more than ever. It has been three years since that loveless night, the last time I saw Marco.

She had forgiven him. She continued to write:

I free myself from all judgment, criticism, guilt and resentment towards myself, towards him and towards his family. I do not want any more drama. I open my heart to joy, to faith in love, to good humour and to the magic of life.

Marco, I forgive you and I release you, because it is the only way I can discover my peace. I thank you for what you gave me and I thank life and God for how I learned to follow my own path. I forgive you for your betrayal and lies.

She knelt beside her bed, in front of a window that overlooked her beautiful garden. It captivated her as she sat and looked.

My bed is empty, yes, but I know myself more than ever. That is priceless. I am enjoying being independent, feeling alive and wanting to move forward. I am not the first woman nor the last to suffer a betrayal by the love of her life. I accept this as it is, and I will continue to live. I have learned who I am, and I recognize myself. I have strengthened my self-esteem and decided to make decisions for myself. I want to love in freedom without being controlled.

I wish you the best, Marco. I hope that you are happy, and that life will smile for you like the stars in heaven. I found it hard to realize that our marriage was not to be forever, as I expected. Our story had a different ending and I had to face it, understand it and accept it. Marco, you were also entitled to end the relationship and make your life apart from me. I will continue my path and continue growing and enjoying the life that God has given me.

Love Knocks at the Door Once More

Knock, knock.

After almost four years, love once again came knocking at Sofia's door, but this time in a different way. With some misunderstanding in the beginning, Sofia gradually became acquainted with a colleague whom she had worked with on several presentations. They exchanged messages about professional interests and before she knew it, a beautiful friendship was emerging.

Rodolfo was a gentleman, understanding, spiritual and always smiling. He was very patient as he began to court Sofia, who remained very reserved. The fear of being hurt again made her cautious. Despite her fear, with the acceptance and the forgiveness she had found, peace shone in her eyes. Sofia prayed, "God, give me wisdom. Open my eyes so that I can discern if this person should have a place in my life or not."

Rodolfo's sincere affection began to make a space in Sofia's heart, which would allow him to enter. He showed her there was a different way of treating your partner —

with love and respect. Rodolfo came from a Christian home, where growth as a person is based on Christ, which is why he seemed to genuinely "love his neighbour." With ongoing respectful treatment, the relationship grew healthy and strong.

Sofia's relationship with Rodolfo became another world for her. It was a free relationship in Jesus, where they did not need to determine who had power over the other or who should be dependent on whom. They simply allowed the relationship to flow, with autonomy. It was built not on material things, but in the bond of spiritual friendship.

One night while eating dinner at a Japanese restaurant, Rodolfo told Sofia that he desired to be more than friends, and he wanted them to be a couple. The trust and sincere affection in his words embraced her, and she bowed her head with a yes. They shared a kiss as they left the restaurant together.

That evening, Sofia wrote in her diary:

Actions are more important than words. The consistency between what he has said and what he has done is what made me trust again.

After three years of dating, Sofia and Rodolfo got married. It was a breathtaking night in the sparkling light of the moon, with the most beloved of both families together in celebration, sharing dinner around a pool with candles, blue hydrangeas and fountains in a capital hotel.

Shortly after getting married, they remodelled Rodolfo's house together. Sofia came to live with her three dogs and four turtles. They gathered what they had in their separate lives and brought it all together to start a new life. "For the first time I have the possibility of creating a home without fear," said Sofia. "In this relationship I can be myself and you can too. I am so grateful."

"I love you Sofia. This is your home, our home and everything is going to be just fine," Rodolfo said hugging her.

Today, Sofia and Rodolfo share a blessed life together. Most mornings Rodolfo prepares breakfast with lots of love and they always pray together. They go to the fair or to the cinema, they talk about their jobs, and they share joy with their families. They both do their part to make a home where they want to be. There have been difficulties just like any other relationship, but they are moving forward. They move forward with love, dialogue, maintaining a good outlook, and most importantly with God at the center of their lives.

CHAPTER 10

Mama and Me

I AM Trisha Ollivierre

The Calm Before the Storm

"It's like looking at my reflection is something I've never done in my life. I don't want to see what he saw," Sarah says as she stares into the pond and watches the ripples take away her reflection. She can feel the fur of her poodle against her left hand. "Hi girl," she says lovingly as she rubs her dog's head and allows the dog's lick to wash away her thoughts. She grabs a stick lying on the ground and tosses it. "FETCH!" The poodle runs and catches the stick before it hits the ground. "Atta girl! Come back now," she calls out as she watches her beloved pet run back to her happily.

Sarah leaves her safe place and heads home. It is getting dark and there aren't any streetlights where she and her little poodle are. As she enters the house, her mother greets her at the front door with bitter words. Sarah tries to dodge every blow but the words seem to slice through her skin. Bit by bit she feels her inner self shrinking.

Where is all this coming from?" she screams at the top of her lungs. The tension in the air is a thick and ever-expanding cloud of darkness.

"Don't you dare talk back to me, Sarah!" her mother yells.

Sarah knows what is coming next. Before violence can erupt, she makes a run for her room. She can hear the stairs bowing to her mother's footsteps behind her. She enters her room and quickly locks the door. "I'm right and you're wrong!" says her mother as she pounds at the door.

Sarah's heartbeat echoes loudly in her ears. *What if she breaks down the door?* The question plays and replays on her mind as she waits. But there is only silence now. *That's unusual,* she thinks to herself.

It's been 30 minutes. Maybe she's gone, Sarah hopes. Gently she turns the nob, but the sound of her door was what her mother was waiting for. Her mother pushes on the door with a toxic rage, but Sarah pushes back with enough force to close the door and lock it.

"Oh God, when will I be safe again?" she cries.

Love with a Twist

Sarah's phone vibrates and she opens it to see a text message from John.

"Hello to the most beautiful girl in the world!" it reads.

"He must be here!" Sarah's face lights up as if it was time to open presents on Christmas Day. She runs down the stairs of her aunt's house. As she turns the nob to go outside, she notices a shadow. It is John. Without hesitation, she throws the door open and jumps all over him. "John!" she squeals. "I am so happy you are here."

Her birthday is this weekend and John has come all the way from England to spend time with her. He makes her feel special like no one else does. For nine years John and Sarah have been best friends. John knows Sarah's darkest secrets and they share a special bond together. They have always been very close, although Sarah's parents know nothing about John. Sarah knows that she likes him, and John shares the same feelings.

"Stunning!" John looks her up and down, "Why don't you wear dresses again?"

"Well, I. . . " she pauses long enough for him to realize she will not finish the sentence.

"Never mind Sarah," John interrupts, "Let's go; I have something to show you."

"OK, let me get my purse and lock up," Sarah says as she re-enters the house and quickly puts on her shoes. As she locks the door behind her, her excitement grows. Spending the evening with John is probably the best thing to happen since her mother went into rehab six months ago and she went to live with her aunt.

John and Sarah drive until they come to a long dirt driveway. John takes Sarah by the hand and they make their way to his family cottage.

Once inside, John gives Sarah the tour and they sit down in the living room on the couch. John and Sarah begin to go through photos of them together that they have taken over the years. As they look through the photos, John's words and his entire body express his love for her. Sarah watches him as the words fall from his lips. As he professes his love for her, she looks into his green eyes and can see the passion burning for her. Sarah takes in the moment slowly. As he speaks, she notices how neatly dressed he is. As she watches his lips move, she is drawn back to the moment of their first meeting.

They were both in a shelter nine years ago. A flashback memory produces vivid images of the bruises that once covered his face. She remembers his clothing ripped up from fighting with his dad that night. Sarah giggles, ever so slightly, as she notices how confident and sure of himself he is now. As she snuggles close and their lips meet, she wonders if this is a dream. Was she actually with the guy she met nine years ago?

John notices the tears running down her face. "Are you OK, Sarah?" he asks.

Sarah turns away quickly. "I just have a little something in my eye . . . that's all."

"Hmm . . . that's what you said last time," John says and then pauses a moment as he considers how to change the subject and ease the discomfort. "It's your birthday and you shouldn't be sad. I hope these are happy tears."

Sarah laughs and says, "Yes, they sure are."

Sarah stands up as she notices the big mirror in front of her. *I still have my baby face,* she thinks to herself.

"You haven't changed a bit," John says as he comes from behind and hugs her. "Maybe if you do this more often you'll see what I see." It is the first time she has seen a mirror in years. Her house was always dark, and its mirrors were smashed at one time or another. Looking at herself is a new venture she isn't sure she can do. She sees her dark brown hair and notices how long it is. She touches her beautiful earrings — her birthday present from her dad when she was four. She has never taken them out. Her light brown eyes match the colour of the choker around her neck. She sees how beautiful she looks in her grey and black dress.

She had sworn she would never wear a dress and here she is standing in front of a mirror, looking at how the dress curves with her body. John stands behind her the whole time because he knows the last time he tried to get her to look at herself, she shook with terror and couldn't do it.

"See, this isn't so bad," he says. Sarah shuts her eyes tight as she remembers why she never wants to look at the mirror in the first place.

"Sarah, it's OK. I'm here. You're OK now," says John as he pulls her away from the mirror. "Come back Sarah," John reassures her. "It's just the two of us now."

But Sarah is already lost to the past. She remembers the night her life turned upside down.

It was a night exactly like this and seven-year-old Sarah Armstrong was standing in her room combing her long, beautiful hair in front of a full-length mirror. She was staying with a foster family after she had been taken from her mother's care.

"Sarah?" someone called out. It was Ray. Ray was one of the uncles in her foster family who lived in the home. He slept in the room across from Sarah, and being the high-spirited young girl she was, she did not take notice of his extra-long glances in her direction.

That night his presence in her room surprised her. All the excitement from her seventh birthday evaporated when suddenly Ray moved towards the light in the middle of the room and unscrewed the light bulb.

"What are you doing?" Sarah asked in the darkness.

"Sarah, you have to do something nice for me and I will give you your light back," he said back to her.

Sarah looked at him with confusion written all over her face. Then she did what every little girl would do when they realize they are stuck in the dark with a monster. Sarah sought refuge under her bed. She understood that "something nice" was not a good thing.

Ray, who wanted what he wanted that night, dragged little Sarah by her hair from under the bed and stood her up in front of the mirror. "If you run from me again, I will kill you," he said. The mirror bore witness to the evil that unfolded that night. Sarah closed her eyes as he undressed her in the mirror. Her entire life changed that night.

The mirror in this cottage forces her to relive the exposure of her little body and the assault. John does not understand the reason for her shaking. He quickly moves to the window and closes it. He pulls a tissue from his pocket and dabs the tears flowing freely down her face. Confused and helpless, he hugs her. Sarah sinks into his arms. Sarah knew looking into the mirror would cut like a razor, but this time she wanted to face her demons. Why is it so hard to cross this bridge? Why does she always have to look away?

"Sarah, are you OK?" John asks.

"Not really, but I will be," she responds. She can at least be truthful with John. Sarah has never told John the full story about why she never looks in mirrors. She is sure he has an idea, but he has never pushed it. She has never told anyone about that night.

"Can we leave and go for ice cream?" Sarah asks in a hoarse voice.

"Sure," says John to oblige her as he warmly kisses her on the cheeks. "Let's go for ice cream."

New Beginnings

John notices Sarah's silence but says nothing. He allows her to just stare out the window as they drive.

"We're here," John announces as he pulls into the parking lot of the ice cream parlour. Sarah's favourite ice cream is a banana split, and without even asking John goes to the counter to buy two banana splits.

Before Sarah and John finish their banana splits, her phone rings. It is her mother. "Hi Sarah, it's mom. Where are you little girl?" her mother asks.

"Hi mom. My friends took me out for ice cream since my birthday is coming up," Sarah lies. She has never told her mother about John. She braces for the rush of anger she has come to expect from her mother.

"Oh yes, that's right. I almost forgot," her mother says and then pauses for a moment. "It might be a little early, but happy birthday, sweetheart!"

Sarah looks at John in amazement. Sarah can't believe her mother said happy birthday. She can't believe she is actually having a normal conversation with her mother.

Her mother continues, "I just wanted to call and tell you that I've arrived home safe and sound."

Sarah sits there and takes it all in. Her mother is finally home after being in rehab for the past six months. She had been fighting her demons for so long that Sarah never thought she would get sober. And yet, she is home and waiting to see Sarah again.

"I'm glad to hear you got home safely, mom. I'll be at the house by 10:00. See you soon," Sarah replies before hanging up the phone.

"So, she has finally done it, Sarah!" John says with a smile. He knew Sarah's mom could get sober, but Sarah had a hard time believing it.

Sarah and John sit and talk about her mother, the treatment centre, and what it has been like living at her aunt's house. Being with John makes her feel safe. Her house was always a battlefield and she didn't know how to not anger her mother. Now that she is back, what will life be like?

John notices the pensive look on Sarah's face as he drives her to her house, and assures her he is just a phone call away. Thank God for John, Sarah thinks as she steps out of the car. The warmth of his embrace disappears when she notices her mother running towards the car. She looks different.

"Mom is that really you?" Sarah returns the hug her mother gives her.

"I'm sorry Sarah," her mother whispers in her ear. "I am so sorry." The words soften the rock that had replaced Sarah's heart. She sinks into her mother's arms and cries.

Everything shifts that evening as Sarah's mom finally tells her daughter her own hidden stories. She tells Sarah of her rape, brutal torture, alcoholism and her new journey toward recovery. This is the first step in her recovery journey: a formal apology to all the people she has hurt. Sarah can't stop the tears as she listens to her mother's horrific experiences. She finally understands why her mother treated her the way she did. She understands the anger; she has felt that same anger herself.

"Sarah, I know it's a lot to take in right now," says her mother, pleading for understanding, "but I hope you can find it in you some day to forgive me."

"I forgive you, mom," she says as they hug again. Three hugs in one day.

On the way up the stairs, she pinches herself. Perhaps this is all a dream. A dream date with John. Mom is home and a changed woman. Isn't this the best birthday ever? Sarah thinks.

Sarah goes into her bedroom, and for the first time in a long time, it looks different. Her bed is made and a journal is on the bed. In it her mom left her a note.

Dear Sarah,

I know I've messed up but I want you to know, I want a better life for us. You are so young, and I promise you, I will stop drinking for you. This journal is for you to write about the pain I caused you and all the times I should have been here for you. I saw your graduation pictures. I'm sorry I wasn't sober enough to attend. Sarah, I'm so sorry and I promise to do better from now on. I'll be there for you if you let me.

Love Mom

New Connection

A week passes and Sarah and her mom slowly begin to mend the hole that has been in their relationship for most of Sarah's life. Sarah sees a new side of her mother that she has never seen before. This brings out a new side to Sarah — a more confident woman that might just be able to speak about her own hidden past.

It is Friday evening and it is Sarah's 16th birthday. Her mother has prepared a special evening for just the two of them at home.

"Sarah! Are you coming down for dinner?" her mom calls out.

"Be there in a minute, mom," Sarah replies. Her mother has purchased a beautiful pink and black dress with matching accessories that she wants Sarah to wear. Sarah inspects the pink shiny shoes on the floor from a distance. Though she is excited, Sarah wonders why her mom wants her to dress up for dinner. Quickly she puts on her dress and glances at herself in the mirror. For the first time, she wants to look good for whatever her mother has planned.

Sarah opens the kitchen door and immediately notices something different. The kitchen has been cleaned and has neatly organized counter tops. Sarah has never seen glass shine so brightly. Her eyes move from the kitchen into the living room. The couch has covers and there is a new space saver with a flat screen TV.

Is this my house? she wonders.

"What took you so long?" her mother says with a smile.

"Mom, what is going on?" Sarah says, smiling back.

"Before rehab, I just wanted to get high and forget about my problems. I only saw how my life was falling apart. I didn't even see my helpless baby girl who needed me.

That is what drugs do to you. They make you forget about your family," Sarah's mother continues without a pause. "It's a new life not just for me, but for you too."

Sarah can't believe these words are actually coming out of her mother's mouth. She stands in shock, praying that after her mom's last sentence she won't wake up from a dream. She does not wish to have her mother change back to the cruel, selfish and overbearing person she knew her whole life.

"Enough about me. You look so beautiful," her mother says, interrupting Sarah's thoughts. "Spin around and let me see you." Sarah's mother's eyes shine with pride as she watches Sarah twirl in the kitchen. "I wasn't sure you would like the colour, but everyone loves pink," she adds, beaming.

"It's beautiful, mom. Thank you so much for the birthday gift," Sarah replies, smiling. In 19 years, this is the only time Sarah can remember getting a gift from her mom.

The table is set for two, with two lit candles sitting at the centre of the small table. The fragrant scent of coconut mixed with vanilla relaxes Sarah. She is so happy to be having a date with her mom after so many years of craving her attention.

"OK, here we are." Sarah's mom places a small roast on the table and quickly goes back to the kitchen. The rice, vegetables and salad follow shortly. Before she sits down, she pours a flavoured drink into both of their glasses. As her mother sits in the seat across from her, Sarah looks deep into her mother's eyes. She can feel the love her mother is putting out. She knows it is real.

"Sarah, close your eyes and let's say a prayer of thanks," her mother requests. "While in rehab they taught me and the other wounded women how to pray. I learned how to thank God for protecting me and ask Him for his guidance. Tonight is a good night to thank him for renewing our relationship and mending our home and our lives."

Sarah closes her eyes and listens to her mother pray. "Dear God, I bring my daughter Sarah and myself before you. I want to thank you for the meal you have provided, thank you for protecting us, and thank you for mending our lives. Amen."

Sarah opens her eyes and feels the tension leave her body. Sarah can't understand what just happened but she knows she enjoys holding her mom's hands.

The phone rings and Sarah springs up from the table to see who it is. On the other end of the line there is a man's voice. "Hello, is Julie there?" he asks.

"Yes, she's home. Just one second," Sarah replies. "Mom the phone is for you."

"Hello?" Sarah's mother says as she picks up the phone.

"Hi Julie, it's Ray. How are you doing this lovely night? I was wondering if you would join me and my daughter Krystal for dessert? It's her birthday today and we are heading out to celebrate," Ray says.

"What a coincidence! It's my girl's birthday too! I haven't told her about you yet, though. It's our mother-daughter night and she's enjoying it. I don't want her to think I'm out to replace her dad. I'll see if I can get her out of the house for some ice cream and we can meet up," Sarah's mother says and smiles.

Sarah hears the end of the conversation and comes over. "Who was that, mom?" she asks.

"Oh, that was my friend Ray," her mother replies. "He is celebrating his daughter's birthday too. What do you think about going out for ice cream after dinner?"

"Sure!" Sarah says with a big smile.

Later that evening, on the way to the ice cream parlour, Sarah gets the courage to tell her mother about John.

"Hey mom," she says cautiously, "there is something I've been meaning to tell you."

"Sure, honey. What is it?" her mother asks.

"Well, there is this guy I like a lot. His name is John and he is the sweetest guy I've ever met. I've known him for nine years. We met in the shelter before I went into foster care, and he promised to keep in touch after his parents came to get him and we did," Sarah says and gazes at her mother to gauge her reaction.

"Oh Sarah, I am so happy to hear this!" her mother says with a smile. Sarah is shocked by her mom's reaction. She is calm and collected, and Sarah has never seen that before.

"Is he a gentleman?" her mother continues.

"Oh yes, he is!" Sarah says, beaming.

"So, when can I meet him?" her mother asks.

"I haven't thought about that yet," Sarah replies.

"Why don't you invite him for dinner on Sunday?" her mother asks. Sarah is so excited to hear this that she texts John right away. She tells him about dinner and that she hopes he can come. John responds almost immediately with "Awesome! See you Sunday night."

Sarah cannot believe this is happening. She feels like things are finally falling into place in her life.

A Blast from the Past

Sarah and her mom enter the ice cream shop and head to the counter to place their order. Once they get their ice cream, they look around the shop for a place to sit. In the back corner there is a man and a young woman sitting in a booth. Sarah's mother immediately walks over and sits down. Sarah follows behind, but when she gets to the booth she stops. She feels as though the air has been sucked out of her lungs. There, sitting in the booth with a big smile on his face, is Ray.

Her mother, completely unaware of Sarah's shock, says, "Sweetheart, this is Ray. He is who I was talking with on the phone earlier tonight. I wanted to tell you earlier, but I couldn't quite find the words. We are seeing each other. He has helped me recover, and he helped me fix up my house and my life. I'm so grateful," she says lovingly towards Ray.

Sarah feels her stomach twirling. Her worst nightmare has become a reality. She begins to feel dizzy and her hands begin to sweat. She drops her ice cream and runs into the ladies' washroom with her mother following behind her. In the washroom Sarah begins hyperventilating and passes out on the floor. Her mother frantically calls an ambulance as she helplessly looks on.

Sarah wakes up a couple of hours later in the hospital with her mother holding her hand. Her mother alerts the nurse that she is awake, and the nurse comes to her bedside.

"Sarah," the nurse says, "you're OK now. You passed out

in the washroom and you're at the hospital. You had a panic attack. Do you remember what happened?"

Sarah does not want to talk so she simply nods her head no, closes her eyes and goes back to sleep. While Sarah sleeps, the nurse reassures her mother that everything is going to be fine. She informs her that they are going to refer Sarah to a psychologist for observation.

A short while later, a woman with golden hair enters the room. She is very tall and wears a black dress with green heels and accessories to match. The noise her shoes make wake up Sarah from her sleep. Sarah knows she isn't alone and opens her eyes to see a woman sitting across from her.

"Hi there. Your doctor told me you might need someone to talk to," the woman says. "Let me introduce myself. My name is Natalie Manning and I'm a counsellor here at the hospital."

Sarah doesn't say anything, so Natalie continues, "The doctor told me you fainted earlier this evening and had what appeared to be an anxiety attack. So, I'm here if you need to talk." Sarah sits up on the bed with her head down and Natalie knows she wants to say something.

"Sarah, take your time. You don't have to do this now if you don't want to," Natalie says as she sits on the chair next to Sarah's bed. Sarah can't hold back the tears.

"Sarah, can you tell me what happened?" Natalie asks.

She holds Sarah's hands and offers her a comforting look. She senses that the answer to her question is something Sarah has kept a secret for a long time. Sarah takes a deep breath and begins to tell Natalie about the horror she has been through.

"Sarah, I'm so sorry." Natalie is physically disturbed by Sarah's story. "No child should have to go through something like that. I want you to know that none of this is your fault and I'm so proud of you for opening up to me."

Natalie assures Sarah that everything will stay between the two of them unless Sarah says otherwise. She promises Sarah that she will be there for her as long as she needs her. Just as they are finishing their conversation, Sarah's mother comes back into the room. Natalie politely excuses herself and slips out of the room without another word.

Fight for Survival

The next evening, Sarah's mother picks her up at the hospital and brings her home. She makes sure Sarah has a shower and makes her some tea. She puts her to bed and lovingly covers her with warm blankets. Then her mother heads across the street to the neighbour's house for a visit, leaving the door unlocked.

A few hours pass and Sarah awakes. She gets up to use the washroom and hears a noise downstairs. She thinks nothing of it and assumes it is her mom getting ready to cook something in the kitchen. She heads back to bed and tries to fall back to sleep.

Suddenly, Sarah hears a noise in the hallway outside her bedroom. She turns over in bed and sees a man standing in her bedroom doorway. Her heart starts beating out of her chest.

"Hi Sarah," the man says.

Sarah feels a lump in her throat. She knows at that moment it is Ray. She is frozen helplessly on the bed as the shadow comes closer.

"You might be wondering how I found you. Well, a few days before your mother went into rehab, she went to a bar. I was also at that bar and she sat down next to me. We started talking and she kept telling me how she was going into rehab soon and wanted to change her life for her daughter. That's when she showed me a picture in her wallet, and I couldn't believe my eyes. There I was looking at a picture of you. I got so excited when I saw your face. But of course, I couldn't let your mother know that I had lived with you all those years ago. I couldn't let her know our little secret. So, I flirted with your mother and swept her off her feet. I knew it was the only way I could see you again."

Sarah begins rising from her bed, but Ray grabs her legs and drags her down the bed. Sarah knocks her head on the ground, and he stands over her and begins ripping off her clothes.

"I love you," he says, "and tonight I'll prove it."

Sarah pulls away from him leaving the clothes in his hands. She rolls under the bed, naked and trying to get away. He grabs her legs and tries to drag her away from the bed but she holds on tightly to the footboard. Frustrated, Ray storms out of her room, leaving Sarah shaking. Sarah waits until she feels it is safe, and she runs to the bathroom to grab a towel. She finds her phone, hides under a table and calls Natalie. When Natalie answers the phone, the only words Sarah can mutter are, "He's here."

Natalie doesn't hesitate and leaves her house immediately. She rushes through traffic and arrives at Sarah's house to find the front door wide open. Natalie runs up the stairs and finds Sarah hiding underneath the table. She tries to get Sarah out from under the table but Sarah screams and cries. Sarah no longer feels like a 19-year-old but rather that little girl in foster care so many years ago.

"Ray was in my room!" Sarah finally manages to choke out. "How am I supposed to tell my mother that her lover is the man who took away my innocence? Would she even believe me? I'm so scared."

"Did he hurt you?" Natalie asks.

"Yes, he did. He ripped off my clothes and he said he wanted to prove he loved me. He grabbed me and dragged me to the floor," Sarah says with tears in her eyes.

After some time, Natalie is able to calm Sarah. Slowly she begins to come towards Natalie and out from under the table. She has been shaken to the core.

Secrets Revealed

An hour later, Sarah's mother comes home from visiting the neighbour across the street. When she steps inside, she notices the light is off and the room is dark. She turns on the light to see Sarah wrapped up in the arms of Natalie on the couch in the living room. Julie can't understand what is happening to her daughter and begins asking many questions.

Natalie knows she has to tell Julie about what happened to Sarah tonight and in foster care in order to protect her and stop this from happening again. She takes a deep breath and begins.

"Julie, Ray is not the man you think he is," Natalie says. "He actually knows Sarah from when she was little. He was a member of the foster family that Sarah stayed with when she was seven. During that time, he took something from Sarah she can never get back. Her pain is so deep.

She didn't tell me exactly what he did to her, but I've heard enough to know that he is dangerous."

I knew something happened to her, but I just didn't know what," Julie says as a wave of sadness and shocked washes over her. "She wasn't happy after she came back from foster care. It was as if she lost her happiness there and she wasn't the same again. She was very angry, moody and she was sad all the time. She never went out with her friends and she began to fail in her classes. She couldn't focus like she used to. I made her do art classes and the teacher said her drawings were dark and she was a very angry child."

"My life was getting out of control and I couldn't help her," her mother continues. "A few days before I went to rehab, I went to a bar and I met Ray. He was so nice to me. He paid for my treatment, and he helped me get better. He talked about marriage and how he wouldn't mind taking care of Sarah even though she was already 19."

Julie is now crying and realizes the danger she put her daughter in. "Did he hurt her?" she asks. Sarah nods slowly.

"Sarah I'm so sorry. I had no idea that Ray is such a monster. I'm the worst mother," her mother sobs.

Natalie embraces Julie and tells her it wasn't her fault. She tells them she will stay with them and help them call the police.

A short while later, the police come to the house to take statements from all three women. Sarah doesn't want to relive her nightmare, but she knows Ray has to be punished for his crimes. With Natalie on her left and her mom on her right, Sarah tells her story. Ray would be arrested later that night.

Captured

Unable to sleep, Sarah takes out the journal her mother gave her. She has yet to write anything in it. She grabs a pen and begins to write.

I've had the most bittersweet week. I celebrated my 19th birthday and was attacked by a pedophile, a man who lived with me years ago. He returned to hurt me, but I am stronger now and fought for my life. He is finally captured and he is nowhere near me to hurt me again. I have to tell John about Ray. I want him to know now what I have gone through. I have a new friend and counsellor named Natalie. She is the only one I truly trust besides John.

Natalie teaches men and women how to handle their problems without drinking too much alcohol and using drugs. She teaches women how to feel better about themselves despite someone harming them by hitting them, calling them hurtful names, and forcing them to do things in their private areas they don't want to do. She helps you to be strong and to fight for yourself. She also helps you to recover.

Natalie helped me to open up and not to be afraid or to keep secrets. I don't know if I will ever have the strength to go over this again in court, but I know with her help I can get past all this mess. I will become someone who can help other people someday.

Mom, I love you. I forgive you. If you could have done this differently, I know you would have.

Judgment day

Sarah awakes to the vibration of her phone. It is reminding her that her court case is in five hours. She covers her head with her pillow, trying to get away from her reality. She thought that because Ray was in prison she wouldn't have to see him ever again. The court case reminds her of how wrong her thoughts were.

"Sarah, it's time to get up," says her mother at her bedroom door.

"Is it time already?" Sarah asks

"No dear, it's time for breakfast," her mother says calmly. Relieved, Sarah gets out from bed and is greeted with hot cocoa and pancakes — her favourite.

Sarah's mother suggests they all wear red at court to show unity; Sarah, her mother and John leave the house wearing red proudly. Sarah feels nauseous and cannot believe she is going to testify against Ray in court.

The drive is long, and when they get to the courthouse, everyone is waiting outside. The lawyer takes Sarah into a room and starts asking questions. The lawyer wants to know if Sarah is strong enough to testify against Ray. Sarah tells the lawyer that although she is scared, she wants to look him in the eye and tell the jury what he did.

"If you change your mind, it would not affect the outcome," the lawyer assures Sarah.

Suddenly, there is a knock on the door. It is time. Sarah's heart is racing but she walks confidently up to the stand. She can't help but notice Ray watching her with his piercing eyes.

While Sarah is speaking, Ray gets up from his seat and shouts, "I did it! I did everything she said."

The judge asks Ray to be quiet and Sarah continues answering the questions. She is strong throughout the whole hearing and in the end the Jury believes her story. Ray pleads guilty and he is sentenced to 15 years in prison.

As Sarah leaves the courthouse, she sees the officers taking Ray away in handcuffs. "You will never have to see him again," a voice says. She turns around to see Natalie standing there, smiling. Natalie hugs Sarah tightly as tears run down her cheeks.

"What's next Sarah?" asks Natalie.

"Oh, that's easy," replies Sarah. "Heal, grow and help others."

New Life

After a couple of group sessions with Natalie, Sarah learns the importance of forgiveness. She also learns that forgiveness is for her healing and not the people who hurt her. The next couple months is very tiring for Sarah because she has to come to terms with the fact that she is a victim of sexual abuse and she also has to learn how to forgive the unforgivable.

After living in denial for so long, she finally admits how traumatic it was for her to go through the whole process. She learns how to accept her emotions and release them through forgiveness.

Later on, she forgives herself for keeping her secret for so long. She also releases Ray and all the memories attached to him.

Sarah is now determined to help other children who experienced similar situations. She joins Natalie in advocacy for abuse teams and she tells her story at every session. She brings hope and healing as she speaks to the victims. She reminds them that they all survived and that they are conquerors.

On her 20th birthday, Sarah and her mom dedicate their lives to Christ and they allow his liquid love to heal their soul, mind and bodies. Sarah makes a pledge to protect the kids of her nation by joining an academy. There she learns the signs and symptoms of children who are living in abusive homes or have experienced earlier abuse. Armed with this knowledge, she is able to identify abusive situations and save children from going through what she did.

Sarah's mother encourages her to apply to a college that is offering degrees in social work and counselling. Although Sarah is still young, her mother knows her daughter's potential. Following her mother's suggestion, Sarah applies to a university in Texas. A few weeks later, she receives a letter announcing her acceptance into the university. She is overjoyed. Sarah and her mom move to Texas to start a new journey together. After years of hard work and dedication, Sarah graduates with her master's in psychology and social work, at the top of her class.

Today, she is continuing her education and in her spare time works with kids ages seven years and older at a centre for abused kids and young adults. She can finally see the beauty in her brokenness as she helps the kids go through their process of healing and forgiveness. By standing up for herself, Sarah now experiences freedom.

She shows other kids the way to freedom by forgiving and loving themselves, regardless of their past. Sarah works towards a brighter future by helping others overcome and forgive — one day at a time.

CHAPTER 11

The Cry of The Children

I AM Marsha Miller

"I choose life!"

My eyes light up as I repeat the words. At first, each word leaves my mouth with halting uncertainty, but soon I am smiling a wide beaming smile. I feel radiant like the sun. My entire being is illuminated in the warmth of its glow.

"I choose a life filled with prosperity and abundance!"

As I speak the words that free me, I stare at myself. I wish that I had known earlier that it all started with me. I wish that someone would have shown me that there was someone who needed me, and that person was myself.

I am standing in my therapist's office, staring at my reflection with tears streaming down my face like a raging waterfall. It is here that I fully understand the purpose of the tiresome and difficult journey that has brought me to this point. It is here that I find my true self, the inner me.

Stories of Triumph

Though my name is Jasmin, everyone called me Jazzy. This is the way it is in Jamaica. Names written on birth certificates are almost always shortened or exchanged for names family members and friends think are more suited to our nature and character.

I woke each morning to the sounds of the roosters crowing and birds chirping merrily from nests hidden in the trees surrounding my home. Early in the morning, I would walk to the back steps and gaze upon the beautiful scenery of my mom cooking fried dumplings and cow's milk over a wood fire, and the sound of my dad moving the animals to the greener pasture. The scenes and sounds were a wondrous joy to me.

I grew up in Middlesex, Jamaica — a tiny, picturesque town nestled at the end of an avenue where bamboo trees stretched for miles to create a canopy that offers cover to passers-by. Middlesex is a sleepy, quaint town with amazing sunrises. Standing on our veranda, I often marvelled at the rows of trees of different shapes and heights that rose majestically from the ground that gave way to beautiful rolling hills. My mother, father and I would play games on the veranda, sometimes making attempts at associating the shapes of the trees and clouds on darker nights with familiar shapes of animals or places. I loved running barefoot outside. Especially in the early mornings, I enjoyed the feeling of the cool, soft grass under my feet. We were simple folks who cared for each other passionately. It was home. It was my sanctuary.

I heard many stories of struggle and triumph from my parents' journey. I heard about how they started with a single room and slowly added to it. Eventually we had two bedrooms, a bathroom, a kitchen, and a living and dining room. Even though we did not have indoor plumbing or electricity, we lived comfortably. My parents' stories taught me about tenacity and showed me how love and partnership can help two people with the same values to overcome the odds against them. In their case, it was the objections of my mother's family. They had been friends in middle school and my mother and father would often play together. My mother's family moved to another city, and though they lived different lives, they kept dreaming of finding each other and later they did!

The fact that my parents built their own home has always filled me with pride. It was filled with love and required much attention for its care. I often had to ensure the tiles shone very brightly. It was my daily task to rub them vigorously with a coconut brush, so that when you looked in from the outside, it seemed as if water had been spilt on it. My room was in the back and was the only room that was not tiled. The outside of the house was not painted. Later, I realized that it was because my parents just didn't have the money at the time to finish the outside.

Despite these shortcomings, no one could tell me that our farmhouse did not rise majestically from the ground. A row of hibiscus flowers on both sides provided a hedge, dividing my father's farmland and creating an area for my friends and me to play. My friends, who lived in neighbouring homes, loved playing outdoors. Laughter spilled from our lips as we ran to catch each other or raced to catch fireflies in the moonlight. On school days, we took stones to fruits when mangoes, June plums, almonds and stinking toe — a smelly, sweet bean covered in a thick yellowish powder — were in season. Raiding the fruit trees was a welcomed distraction from the hot and tiring walk home. The juice of the mangoes would stream down our hands and mouth, and we were often in trouble with our parents for staining our school uniforms.

In the mornings ,when I was not running to school or church, I would lie quietly under a tree and listen to the birdsongs . At the back of the house were several mango trees, with roots growing so large over time that they popped out of the earth. My father built me a swing on one of the mango trees, and it is still there to this day.

The Stage is Set

My mom is a hard worker, perhaps one of the most hardworking, kind, loving and determined women that I know. Life was happy and idyllic for me, but I soon became aware of the financial challenges my parents were facing. One egg would be shared between my dad, my sister and I. My mom would not have any of the egg. When we had meat, she gave the best portions to us and dad, and kept the bony parts for herself. I was attached to my mom, forever at her side or resting on her. I remember hearing my parents speaking in very hush tones of the hardship in the wee hours of the night.

"But babe, the pickney dem getting older and you have no job since redundancy," I heard my mom's voice pleading. I didn't quite understand the word redundancy, but I figured it was because daddy was not working outside the home.

"We need to take better care of these girls," she said.

My dad would get mad. My mother was a little afraid of my dad, and we all knew that he had a temper. He would say, "Mi no want you to work. It's my job to take care of my family." My dad had worked as a manager on Appleton Estate, ensuring the 100 proof Jamaican Rum was made to the correct standard. He was a very proud man and wanted to provide for his family. He worked daily on the farm as a substitute, but times were getting hard.

On Sundays, I would often cry to my mom about having soup with no meat for dinner.

"Mom," I cried, "I don't want this. It's Sunday! I want chicken! Everybody else has chicken and rice for dinner."

"It's OK, Jazzy!" she said as she gave me a comforting hug. "Eat it for mommy. One day it will be betta than today!" I could not be comforted. I reluctantly ate the soup. I hated pea soup and I wanted a nice chicken dinner like every other household in the community.

The conversations became constantly more heated and finally, in an attempt to make more money for the family, my mother started working away from home. I saw her every other weekend, but I missed her so much. I cried often as the feelings of abandonment and loneliness grew. My mom had long been my comfort, my refuge and my strength.

I was unprepared for the drastic change to my parent's roles. While my mom worked as a caregiver in the city, my dad tried to take on her roles. My dad worked on the farm as he also took on the role of caregiver, cook and homemaker. After mommy moved to the city, whether by design or coincidence, a series of events were set in motion that would scar me for life.

Darkness

One day, when I was six years old, I was walking home

from school by myself. If I were to think about the atmosphere that day, I would say there were ominous dark clouds on the horizon as I approached the cemetery.

As I walked, I noticed a teenaged boy who was setting a trap for birds. He was about 17 years old and was making a sweep, which is a homemade trap to catch birds. As I passed, he noticed me and called out to me. He had frequented my home before and was well known to me and my family.

I knew what the rules were: Mama often told me to not talk to strangers, to never go into anyone's house, to not take food from anyone and to always walk along the main road. I had always wondered why, and this day — the day I chose to break one of the rules — I learned the reason why.

"Jazzy!" he called as I passed. "Want to see how I catch birds?"

I looked at him and became even more interested as he excitedly waved me over. Always an incredibly inquisitive child, I ambled over with curiosity and proceeded to pepper him with questions.

"What are you doing?" I asked.

"Catching birds," he answered, his tone and demeanour friendly. "Want to see my trap? Want to see how it works?" He spoke in sharp and abrupt sentences.

"How does this work?" I asked warily as I stepped a bit closer. I looked back to the road; I really wanted to visit my Auntie Pearl before heading home.

"You bend the branches together like this," he said and proceeded to show me.

He then asked me to help him hold the branches while he tied them together. I nodded and slowly moved closer to him with a million questions flying through my mind. I could smell the sweat; he must have been at this for a while. He took up the trap, and I could feel the wetness of the mulch on the ground under my feet. A big mango tree was behind me, and there were some graves around us. I did not like the cemetery. He was bending over some shrubs, and I bent beside him to look at how he twisted and bent the limbs to make a trap that would snap down on the legs or neck of a bird. I heard a Barbie dove coo above as the leaves rattled and the wind picked up a bit.

I took a closer look at the trap and asked, "So this is how the birds are caught?"

"Yes!" he said.

I wondered how much longer it would be before the process would end. I had to get home before my dad did, and I told him that. He finished tying, and I started to move back to leave. Then, suddenly, his hand shot up and grabbed me and pushed me back to the tree.

I screamed and screamed. I pushed and screamed. He pushed his hand over my mouth and told me to stop screaming. I bit his hand, but he pressed on my throat even harder. I could not breathe! His eyes hardened as he told me that if anyone heard that they would blame me. He told me that my dad would beat me. He told me that it would hurt less if I moved with him.

Pain after pain assaulted me, and as I closed my eyes, I saw a yellow and black monarch flying above towards the sunlight. The hand that was over my mouth was forcibly slamming the screams back down my throat. I screamed and screamed, but this time on the inside and sobbed quietly. Each motion rocked me into torment but no one heard me. I died that day.

Spent, he released me finally. I was not fighting anymore. Tears streamed down my face and I watched silently as the butterfly fluttered above me.

He told me not to tell, that my dad would kill me with a beating. I had clammed up as soon as he mentioned my father. Would he blame me and beat me for this? What had I done? What have I done?

I looked at him unable to move. He had pulled up his pants and I watched him pull up the trap. I stood there motionless with my underwear at my feet. He turned to walk away, but before he left he said, "You know, your dad is going to think that you are a bad girl. You will get killed with a beating!"

I stood there motionless, frightened, weak and broken. I didn't quite catch the significance at the time, but my therapist pointed out to me that his trap had caught me. The trap was used for two purposes: for birds and to lure little girls.

He walked away and left me standing there with my back to the tree. I waited until he was nowhere in sight and I slowly pulled up my underwear and smooth out my uniform. With my body racked by pain and shame, I ran home. I ran past the mango trees, past the graves, and past my godmother and auntie's house. Her sweet meal was no longer of interest to me. No one saw me that day and that's how I wanted it. I wanted to disappear.

There was no joy when the birds chirped or when my dogs greeted me at the front door. I bathed quickly to ensure that my dad would not bathe me that evening. I didn't want anyone to see the blood or the shame on my face.

I stepped into my room at the back of the house, and I felt sick to my stomach and went to lie on the bed. I curled up in a ball with my hands wrapped around my knees, shaking violently back and forth as I tried to comfort myself. I felt numb with the pain. The bed frame creaked as I shook and cried hot, burning tears.

"I want my mommy! I want my mommy!" I cried. I was still a baby. As I cried, I remembered that my mother worked away from home. I became angry at her for leaving me. I felt like one of the butterflies that my friends and I played with, that could not fly as its wing was crushed.

"How could he do this? I trusted him. Why did he hurt me?" I could not understand as he had always been so nice to me before. Thought after thought jumbled and challenged me. I was his friend — wasn't he my friend? He was the friend who played catch or gave me mangoes when he passed. It did not make sense; this was someone that I knew, whom my family trusted.

"Why did I walk that way?"

"Am I a bad girl now?"

Suddenly, I heard a sound in the house. "Jazzy! Jazzy! Are you home?" My father's voice came through the middle of the questions in my mind, rescuing me.

"Yes, daddy!" I said

"Come and tell me about your day," he said.

"I had a good day, daddy!" I lied.

I slowly pulled myself off the bed and pasted a smile on my face. That was the first time I realized the cruelty of the world as I slid into my façade of the happy-go-lucky daughter and friend.

Lost and Unfound

I was never the same after that day. Could people see that I was not all right? This was my constant fear. Maybe if mom was home, I would have told her. Since mom came home every two weekends, I resolved to bear the burden and not tell anyone about it. I did not want to spoil their fun. This decision ate me up inside; no child should bear this burden alone. I did not want to live anymore, and I felt different. I felt as though I was an incomplete human being. My smile did not light up my eyes; the butterflies, fireflies and my friends did not bring as much joy.

I would often ask myself, "Why did this happen to me? Why didn't I listen? Why did I walk that way?" I concluded that I was a bad girl. I was a failure. The thoughts were strong and convinced me that I deserved what happened. These questions and false beliefs created by my six-year-old mind created a prison that that keep me always gasping for breath.

I remember so vividly the next incident with him. My dad was on the steps washing clothes to hang on the line to dry. As he threw the water on the ground, the butterflies started to gather. I stood in silence, watching as they landed, but I did not chase them anymore. Suddenly the dogs began to bark.

"Hold on dog! Uncle it's me!" Bold like a peacock, he sauntered into the yard like he had done nothing wrong. It had been three months since he had raped me. He had waited to be caught, but nothing happened and now he was here at my home! My dad just sat on the steps washing, with the impression that he was just the innocent family friend bringing us fruits. After exchanging pleasantries with each other, he looked at me and said, "Uncle, can I push Jazzy in the swing?" My dad looked up, and after a moment's pause, told him yes. My dad is normally extremely protective of me. As he walked towards me, I silently prayed for him to trip over the roots of the mango tree. I sat in the swing alone and he pushed me. I wanted my dad to say no, but since he was outside, I was not worried.

Later, he sat in the swing. After a few minutes of swinging alone, he asked daddy again, "Uncle, can I swing with her?" He lifted me up, placing my legs around his waist. I looked at my dad, screaming inside, but the words never came. Tears flowed to my eyes, but my eyes stayed dry. I learned to cry inside. His clothes were on and so were mine, but I felt so violated.

"How could he allow him to put me on his lap and swing with me?" I thought. My dad only saw me as a baby, but this predator did not care. I felt molested in my own home and in front of the person I thought would have protected me with his own life. For sure if my dad had known, he would have killed him that day.

I never spoke about this and it became a prison in which I was bound. I lived in fear and anger. Every day that I had to pass the street where he lived, I would be filled with dread. I would literally run past his house. I wanted to forget. I pretended to be normal, yet the pain was a constant reminder of the trauma. Soon I tried to bury the pain by pushing the memories to the far reaches of my mind. Life went on, one day at a time. As each day began, I woke up still alive, but I went through the usual routine of living while being dead inside.

Later, I learned that he had raped another little girl; it was my friend who lived down the street. After hearing this horror, I no longer cared about getting beaten. I told my parents, and my dad was so furious! He went to speak to his parents but I don't know what was said. The predator spent years in jail but not for what he did to me. My parents never spoke about what happened again; I think they were trying to protect me. However, I never forgot the pain.

The Torment of Fear

At nine years old, I passed my exams for entrance to a prestigious all-girls school called Hampton. Hampton is the best in the country, and I couldn't believe that I had passed! I had worked hard to make my parents proud, despite feeling like I was just going through the motions day to day. I was one of the first girls from my village to go to Hampton in a long time. My dad was so proud that he told whomever would listen about his good news, "my girl is going to Hampton!". My mom's face shone with exuberance and pride when she looked at me.

We soon went to the school, far up on a mountain. I hung my head out the window while marvelling at the sights. As we drove along the red dirt, I suddenly got a glimpse of my school standing in the distance with pine trees lining the long, curved driveway.

It was orientation day. I watched as the girls in their blue and white uniforms came on stage. Mom and I were not prepared for the list of supplies I needed for my stay including blankets and jackets for the very cold nights. Here I was, the daughter of a farmer and a homemaker, among a group of young ladies who were much wealthier than me. I was determined to make my mother proud. I was happy, scared, anxious and excited all at once.

I felt different in high school; I was shy and withdrawn. I sat at the back of the class, and fear was my closest companion. I was afraid to say the wrong thing, and I said not a word unless called upon. I travelled with concealed anger that erupted at my classmates for simple things such as someone bumping into me or someone taking a miniature microscope from me. I was living in pain and it became my identity. Although I was excited that I was there, the experience intensified my isolation and the overall pain of my existence. I felt unworthy, that I was unloved and that I was not good enough. Although I survived high school, being without the comfort of my loving home, it affected me gravely.

I tormented myself often, and I would go back and forth thinking of the worst possible outcomes in my life. I thought that I was the only one going through that experience. I remember thinking that these other girls have not been through the experience of being raped. I thought about how no man would want to marry me. Would someone want to marry a woman who was not a virgin? These thoughts became a daily torture.

On my very hard days, my upbringing actually saved me. I had several occasions where I would get so depressed that I would lock myself away for two days or more and would not eat food. I became suicidal; however, my thoughts about God and my mother saved me.

One of my best friends, Lina, would go to the cafeteria and bring the meals and leave it at the door. Those days, I wanted no contact with anyone as I tried to work through my issues of inadequacy. I would remember my mom and her love and sacrifice, and I would pray for her. Then I would tell myself, "I can do all things through Christ with the utmost courage and courtesy," in order to pull me back from the wilderness in my mind. Then I would get back to studying.

Angel of Light

During my last two years of high school, an angel appeared. She came when all the negative thoughts completely consumed me and kept me locked in a dark prison of pain. Her name was Star, and she was a confident, beautiful, smart girl with a positive attitude. She had an exuberant personality and laugh — she was just different. Whenever I would lock myself away, Star would not let me wallow in my self-pity.

"Get up!" she would say. She would not listen to my cry to be left alone.

Those were the days that depression and suicide would attempt to steal me away from my destiny. But there was Star, encouraging me and telling me, "Let's go!"

If I locked myself away on Friday, by the time Monday came, she would literally climb over the walls of the cubicle to see me. She would lie in my bed with me and tease the hell out of me.

At first, as I struggled with myself, I tested her love. I remember telling her that I had a weird disease just to push her away from me. She cried tears and told me,

"Jazzy it does not matter. I care about you, and if you are sick, I will be here for you." She showed me love, and she understood me.

One day, I finally told Star what happened when I was six, and she cried for me. Later she wrote me a beautiful poem. She walked into my dorm the following Monday and told me that she had been thinking about all that I said, and then she handed me this poem. The first few lines are etched in my memories:

Love yourself
The way you are
Accept the uniqueness of you
God has made
No one else
As special and as unique as you.

As I read it, I could not help but cry. This moment changed me. I started to see myself as not just a rape victim. This was when it all started — my journey to love. I think God sent her to that school just for me, as she died from cancer two years after high school. I have never been able to forget her. She was my angel.

Becoming Me Again

Years later, I finally dealt with my pain in a counsellor's office. She made me look at myself in a mirror, as she brought me back to the day of the event. She asked me to speak to the young man who had taken my innocence. I screamed like I was unable to do on that ill-fated day. I cried for being too small and helpless; I cried for my future and how the tragedy changed the trajectory of my life. My life changed course that day in that cemetery, and the person I was born to be died.

It took me 32 years to get here. I wish I had known earlier the things that I know now. I know now that it starts with me. As someone who has gone through trauma, I remind myself just how uniquely I am created. God never makes a mistake and no, he did not want that tragedy and trauma to happen. I finally feel free. Today, I live my life as the best version of myself.

I know that the journey does not end here. I know that there are cries of many voiceless boys and girls who have been victimized by the simple fact of being in the wrong place at the wrong time. Many who have felt unloved and unwanted, whether because of their gender or even sometimes because of the parents' decisions.

As victims, too many of us protect those who took our dignity from us; too many of us protect the status of our parents. There are parents who refuse to believe what their child is saying because it is an inconvenient truth.

If I could go back and talk with my younger self, I would say: There is nothing you could have done, no other road you could have taken, nothing. You were the victim. For years, I had pondered whether things would have been different if I took the longer route home. For years I tortured myself with the different possibilities. These thoughts made me feel unlovable, incomplete, like a failure, and a disappointment to my family. With the grace of God, I now realize that there was absolutely nothing that I could have done to prevent the predator from taking advantage of me.

I encourage anyone who has experienced this kind of sexual abuse to speak out. The silence does not protect you, it protects the perpetrator who will go on to abuse others. You are thinking of the shame and humiliation, but your healing is more important. You are not alone. You are a survivor. This does not define you! You are more than this circumstance; you survived. You are a victor, not a victim.

I recognize now the purpose for my pain. My goal is to help others to prevent violence and to help those hurting to heal. It's a journey and I am finally letting go of the pain and the hurt. I am letting go of the shame and the fear which had tethered me to my past. I am here, I am still standing, and I am still fighting.

To all the parents:

There are so many lives broken as a result of other broken people who take without caring. Listen to your children;

really listen and address the issues of sexual molestation and rape. Take the time to really know your children. Take notice of the differences in their behaviour. Notice when they are unusually withdrawn.

Build a relationship where your children will feel comfortable in sharing even the most difficult news. Let them know that you love them unconditionally. Write them a note or poem if it's too difficult to open up. If there is an issue of violence, sexual or otherwise, please seek professional help.

I know it's difficult, especially when it comes to reporting something. You may fear the embarrassment but the cost to be silent is so much higher. Some of the more tragic and painful parts of my struggles were depression and sharp anxiety attacks that surfaced later in my life as a result of the trauma I kept secret.

Reassure them that the rape and trauma are not who they are. This is very important. The way I saw myself affected all the relationships that I had, especially the one I had with myself. I never loved myself. I loved others and poured this into them, but I was on the back burner of my own life. Today, I focus on me with the understanding that when I do, I am better able to affect positive changes in the people around me.

I am convinced that I have the love of God, which is

the most complete love of all. Through counselling, in particular forgiveness therapy, my relationship with God has grown. I recognize and accept my completeness in Him. I am complete in His love; I am uniquely created. God has given me the necessary grit to fight, and I never stopped fighting. The poem my best friend wrote back then, finally makes sense to me now. I am unique and created for a special purpose. So are you. It does not matter what your circumstances look like, or whether you have been hurt and rejected. Just know that what it takes to move forward is a belief in yourself. I believe in you.

CHAPTER 12

Undercurrents Within

I AM Angelique Benois

Trust…It is Already There

"What I am looking for is not out there, it is in me."
— Helen Keller

I saw red as I forced my car back into the lane. "Hold on," I thought to myself, "where are they going?" I couldn't think fast enough to analyze what the person in the car in front of me was doing. I felt the stiffness of fear spread rapidly through my body. I knew we were going to collide. I heard my gasp and felt the panic deep in my chest and the rigour in both my arms.

The impact from the car hitting mine caused me to momentarily lose control. I quickly glanced in my review mirror and saw large, bright lights. The initial impact pushed me into the lane to the left of me and I could not stop it. There was the sound of crushing metal and breaking glass, and then I was spit back across to my lane again — this time hitting another car. Time stood still. I heard nothing as many life events began flashing in front of my mind's eye.

Faded Memories

"Sometimes painful things can teach us lessons that we didn't think we needed to know." — Unknown

A memory flashed before me from Grade 3 or perhaps Grade 4. I had left my classroom for some reason that is both unclear and irrelevant. The hallway floors were lit up with light streaming through a large and looming window at the end of the hall. The warmth of the sunshine cast layers of colour, creating a soothing and inviting atmosphere. I looked to my right and noticed a conversation that was unfolding. I noticed a little girl, my friend Rhonda, who was standing awkwardly. From where I stood I could not hear anything, but I felt her discomfort and hesitation through her nervous body movements. The conversation that was unfolding was making her feel something inside her body, which was uncomfortable for me to watch.

The moment was so intense, neither Rhonda nor the teacher noticed my presence. The teacher stood in front of

Rhonda gently coaxing her to speak her truth with a look so kind, yet so concerned. I became nervous with Rhonda. My heart grew and took up space in my throat.

I always knew something was wrong when I played with Rhonda. She always had a smile and was fun to play with, but there was always a sense that something was not right. It was like she wore an invisible shackle, a burden too heavy for any child to carry. As I looked at her in that moment, I felt such sorrow. I saw the shackles for what they were. They were all lies: "I am not good." "I am unlovable." "I am unworthy. . . ." I heard the inaudible scream that echoed from this little girl's heart: "Please, I am begging you . . . help me."

Rhonda brought her hands to her face to hide fresh tears. Like curtains, her dirty blonde hair folded around her face as she bowed and sobbed. I watched the teacher hold her and wait patiently. Finally, Rhonda raised her head and told her story. This poor little girl was raped by her stepfather. Rhonda was surrounded by something vile and unfair. I sensed it whenever we played together. Why didn't anyone else notice this? How could no one else notice this? For years, I wished I could have protected her.

It is interesting how our mind can bring us to a place of blame and self-criticism. It is even more interesting that it is not until later on in life when an experience reveals the connection of different life experiences to one another. Like a hidden message in a bottle, a new discovery is washed to shore for us to view.

I never knew that this would be one of my earliest introductions to the raw impact of sexual trauma. I was sensitive — I still am — but I had to learn from a young age that I had to let go of what I could not control. Life always directed me to these self-care opportunities, and I did them without completely understanding their relevance to my existence. They moulded me, guided me, and saved me. Now that I am wiser, I intentionally invest in ways of being committed to cultivating this mindset.

This memory of Rhonda, this distant vision, was the last I saw of her. No goodbyes, no consoling. I was left with playful memories of special times, then silence and shiny hallway floors. The memory faded like a rock skipped across the water's surface, slowly sinking into the sand below.

My Good Friend Named Vulnerability

"When I stop struggling, I float. It is the law." — *Unknown*

My mind shifted to another significant memory. I had stepped off the elevator and started to walk down the green patterned hallway to my home. My 10-year-old mind couldn't decipher the interesting smells in the hallway, but they lulled me into thoughts about what mom had left me for lunch.

It was my routine to walk home at lunch time and enjoy my lunch as I watched Leave it to Beaver and Three's Company before returning to school in the afternoon. But as I came to my door, something strange was at play. Something was unfamiliar and my heart began pounding in my chest.

The door to the apartment was open. From where I stood in the hallway, I could see part of our living room. The floor was draped by a large vintage rug with rich, vibrant hues and intricate handwoven art. The rug was something that had always given my mother pride in the look and style of the apartment. I glimpsed at the television and I noticed the empty space where our stereo system usually sat.

"Tiny?" I spoke softly, knowing that my dog would hear me. She was always behind the door waiting for me to come home. There was only silence, no whimpering or barking. An anxious heat grew in my stomach and rose into my throat. I could not breathe.

"Tiny?" I said louder. She was not there. Where is she? What is happening?

As I ran for the stairs, I could hardly breathe, not due to exhaustion but because of the effort it was taking to keep the tears at bay. Then I began to cry. I did not know exactly why I was crying, which grew my confusion. I tripped over my feet a few times as I couldn't seem to climb the stairs fast enough. Fear took over. As I made my way to the 15th floor, my tears blurred my vision and it became hard to see the flight of stairs. I was terrified and my heart was beating so fast, it felt like it was going to burst through my chest.

I made my way to my friend Natasha's door and knocked frantically. Natasha came home for lunch too and I knew her family would help me. The moment I saw Natasha and her mom, a wave of relief washed over me. Through my tears I told them that something was wrong and that someone went into or is in my apartment. Natasha and her mom hugged me. Her mom encouraged me to sit down and her dad made the call to the police. I was still afraid and believed this feeling of safety was only temporary.

Several apartments were robbed that same day. They had somehow locked Tiny in the bathroom and quietly removed the items from the apartment. They were so quiet that it did not disturb my older brother who was fast asleep in his bedroom. They took many of our electronics, but that inconvenience did not compare to the feeling of safety being ripped away from me. Walking to go play outside or walking my dog made me wonder if someone was watching me. I knew there was the possibility I could be walking past the thieves on the street and be none the wiser. I felt so vulnerable.

My parents felt unsafe too; I could feel it within them. The robbery would become the driving force behind our move.

The memory shifted to one year later. Despite our attempt to find security and safety, invasion followed us. In my mind's eye I could see myself as I stood with my mother looking out her bedroom window. The entire house had a heaviness to it and my mom's face told me that something was wrong. With her towel wrapped around her naked body, she walked into the room that is directly across from the bathroom. The curtain was blowing, and the hardwood felt cooler than usual. As though wanting to touch something she knew should be present, she stretched out her right hand and moved it through the space where the window screen would normally sit. As the reality of the situation hit her, her eyes widened. The house had been robbed while my mother was in the shower.

I left my mother for a moment and went to my room. As I entered my room, I saw my underwear drawer in a mess. My personal items, my diary and my pictures were all scattered. My jewelry box laid there empty.

"They touched my panties," I cried. "Why did this happen again?"

The same feelings returned. I felt utterly violated and so did my mother. My mom was home alone and in such a vulnerable state when strangers came into our home and stole our property. I felt cold as if I had entered the deep water of the ocean.

Imagine closing your eyes with me. You are floating on your back in the ocean, feeling the water surround you and flowing over the surface of your skin. You can feel the heat of the sun on your face. Through the thin skin of your eyelids you notice the brightness of the sun has faded. You decide to look up and you no longer see the shoreline. The shallow water which you could look down into and view the bottom is now a deep, dark blue, offering you nowhere to securely stand.

Perhaps there has been a life experience which has left you feeling this type of vulnerability. Two home invasions within a short period of time may not seem like a significant deal to many, but as a young girl it confused me. For the longest time I always felt as if I was pulled far away from the shore with my feet dangling beneath me. I was not able to trust the world as I once did. I felt that I was always waiting; I was waiting to be invaded or have my loved one's home invaded. It was such a destructive way of being.

Something positive would happen in my life and then I would tell myself, "Okay, things are going well, so here comes the bad." I was so hypervigilant and guarded. I became very sensitive to how much I disliked the feeling of vulnerability.

Fast forward 30 years and now I welcome the passive pull of life and surrender to not feeling solid ground. When at the beach on vacation, I often challenge myself to stand solid as the sand sucks my feet deeper and leaves me unbalanced. I merge into the water, flip onto my back and just float. I love the feeling of knowing that when I decide to open my eyes and look up, I will not be in the same place.

This experience in my childhood changed me. It created a deep feeling in me, one which I was denying but could not ignore forever. Vulnerability is part of it all. Embracing it builds courage. Denying it builds fear that will just cause one to drown.

Ripples Flow

The flashback shifted to a different memory. I was anxiously waiting at home with a heavy heart. My throat felt dry. The phone rang and I brought the receiver to my ear with hesitation, repeating to myself, "Please let him be okay. Please God." There had been nights where we did not know where my nephew was, and this was one of those nights. The unfamiliar male voice indicated to me that my "son" was found sleeping in the lobby of a condominium and he had no shoes.

I was exhausted from being up all night. I hardly slept and when I did manage to sleep it was of such poor quality I could hardly consider it really sleeping at all. The love I had for him grabbed hold of my feet and directed me to my car to go pick him up. I drove to this unfamiliar place practising in my mind the conversation I would have with him to convince him he should go to the hospital.

This yo-yo ride of uncertainty was exhausting, but my nephew was an amazing person and I could not give up on him. He was affectionate, bright, caring and curious about life. Perhaps too curious. He was experimenting with substances and mixing with an older (but not wiser) crowd.

With him sitting in my car, we made small talk as I tried to discover how he was doing. When I looked deep into his eyes, they seemed to ask the questions: "Will I ever get any better? Will I ever find peace and a clear direction?" The power of mental illness is so strong it touches each person's soul uniquely. The unnecessary shame felt by our family led us to look for someone to blame. But all we really did was hurt one another. As I sat with him, I felt so guilty. I was constantly struggling to do more and yet the more I tried to sort it all out, the more helpless I felt.

Another memory moved into my mind, which took place a few years prior. I gazed at the words on a page that read, "All a youth needs is one consistent person to show unconditional love and it can positively alter their trajectory in life." I agreed with the statement, but I had just made the decision to go overseas. I wondered how my leaving would impact him. The guilt came in full force.

But even in this state, as soon as I noticed this emotion, I buried it. If I thought about it, I would have to feel it. I did a very good job convincing myself that it was not something I had enough strength or energy to do. Though it was not the best choice, I committed to my decision anyway and continued to bury.

Witnessing how this impacted my family stifled me and made it hard to breathe. I watched my nephew and could not stop trying to imagine the defeat he must have felt. When I was with him, I could feel his disbelief that things would get better; the weight of his hopelessness was like a thick, rusted anchor. As he bobbed up and down at the surface, his thoughts regarding his situation kept him in one place. He needed to detach from the anchor, but he kept it. It was always with him.

Even though I knew I was not the only person who has experienced emotional pain and disbelief, it at times felt that way. I was the mental health expert within the family, and this carried such an unnecessary weight of guilt for me. As painful as it was, this experience allowed me to birth a new understanding of how ignoring my pain was not the way I wanted to continue to live my life. I started to see my pain much like a puddle evaporating on a hot summer's day — not simply disappearing but transforming into something else. The pain shifted elsewhere within my body and it patiently waited for a time to slowly maneuver into my other life experiences. Then it would show itself, angrier and louder than before.

I used to reflect on my family situation and tears would well up in my eyes. I would become fearful that if I allowed the flow to start, the flow would never stop. I feared what would surface and show itself. But one day I allowed it to flow out, and in that moment I learned that the flow is not unending and infinite. At some point a good cry comes to an end. It's not that we should force the process to end, but rather it has a natural end.

We Are in the Same Ocean

My mind shifted again. I noticed the fine, soft hairs on my fingers and the way my skin wrinkled at each one of my knuckles as I widely spread my fingers. I felt the resistance between the soles of my feet against the rubber of my yoga mat. My hair gently tickled the side of my face as it slipped from behind my ears and fell to the sides of my face. I pressed and pushed downward into my mat and into my being. I made a small adjustment which deepened my breath and as I moved through the flow on my yoga mat, I experienced a secondary flow of tears. As I allowed them to be released, I shifted deeper into my asana, flowing into the next posture without much effort and sinking deeper into the moment. This experience comforted me. Allowing that energy to be released created a space for me to allow new emotions to flow in and to be felt. Slowly I started to experience forgiveness, acceptance and comfort in trusting that everything occurring within my family was happening for a reason. I learned to let go of the guilt I was holding onto. Allowing this helped me to change the relationship I had with my experiences and to notice all of the undercurrents which were part of it.

This personal life experience positively impacted my professional life as I related to my clients differently. It refined the very thing we all yearn for: connection. Even though I always took great pride in my ability to engage with each of my clients, it was experiencing this connection with myself which created room for an even deeper connection. I was now among the group who have had mental illness impact their lives personally. It was beyond reading about it in books. This pain was real within me. I felt the damage it created, the silent loud rejection it produces and the infectious shame it interjects into so many lives. It is a feeling which resides in me as a reminder that pain teaches us amazing things about life. When I was able to embrace this pain, it revealed who I was in a complete way, and as a result the people I served saw and felt me more deeply.

Now my nephew is healthy, stable and seems to have entered his own state of acceptance. I am eternally grateful for his transformation. I look back at those moments and inspect the mental image of my family drowning in pain.

Everyone frantically reaching for and grasping the person closest to them in a panic, hoping they have found the person with the lifejacket.

However, I cannot ignore the judgments; their presence created a barrier to responding towards each other with empathy. Each person convinced themselves that their wave of pain was larger than everyone else's and forgot we are all in the same ocean of turmoil. Pain has a powerful way of causing these types of illusions and delusions.

Having the opportunity to speak with my nephew regarding his experience was also a life lesson I cannot avoid sharing with anyone who wants to learn from the authentic experience of coping with the direct painful confusion of a mental illness. I sat and not only listened to his responses to my questions, I heard them with my heart and they left a footprint on my soul.

My nephew recalls that his "gratitude, prayer and positive thoughts" helped him remain aware of his true reality. I commend him on finding gratitude within his pain; it is a strength not all of us realize we have access to.

His final teaching was that "if a person does not believe in anything" (meaning a God, a divine or supreme being, something bigger than us) . . . it is a good time to start to believe in something." He viewed the reminders of his self-love and family as gifts offered from God to him, which "help me to push through it all."

This experience taught me to just be present. Be love. Be honest. Be true. I have every reason to believe that I did enough because my nephew felt what mattered — my unconditional love for him. He knew I would always advise, listen, advocate and act in a way with his best intentions at the core of everything I offered. We were all doing the best we could do in that moment in time. It feels as if that chapter in our family's life has been gently shut. I pray for it to be. I breathe that belief in, but I know that if the unexpected happens again, this past experience birthed my new understanding of the word "connection." It guided me to experience connection with myself and others differently and objectively. It is this very element which started to deteriorate in my later years working within the corporate environment. It is this element which my daughter inserted into me when I looked into her eyes and heard the surprising things she has noticed about life within her limited five years. I am present enough to notice, feel and release whatever flows my way and am ready to discover new depths.

Loss and Opportunity

"The foot feels the foot when it touches the ground."
— Unknown

My mind shifted to another memory. I climbed the stairs to my bedroom, slowly walked across my bedroom carpet, and sat at the edge of my bed. "Oh, tonight's sleep is going to feel so good," I said with a smile. I reached for my phone to make sure my alarm was set correctly and to set the phone to flight mode. I noticed a message waiting for me. I saw an image of my favourite cousin on the screen. As I began to read, I remember thinking it was strange that his sister was sending me a text message from his phone. My hands began to tremble. The phone began to feel incredibly heavy and the screen started to blur. My cousin was dead. "I should have done more," I cried. An image of his joyful face, amazing smile and sincere love brought me to tears. I tasted the salt on my lips and dropped my phone.

My cousin's death was a shock to me, not because he had no health concerns, but because of his fighting spirit. I always imagined he would continue to manage with his "never-give-up" mindset. I shared face time with him a couple weeks prior and had left several voice messages which he never returned. "Maybe he needs space. We all need space at times," I convinced myself when I did not hear back. He had diabetes and was experiencing inflammation in his legs. He had fallen down the stairs and this caused him to be bedridden. The stress of it all increased his blood sugar level and his heart could not manage it any longer. For days after I prayed that he was able to say all he needed to say to the people he had to say it to.

One night, I took a walk by myself. Stillness surrounded me and I felt no fear walking alone this particular night.

I noticed it growing inside me: thoughts that I should have checked in with him more, offered more self-care health tips, that somehow I did not do enough. The guilt started to burn my stomach and I noticed feelings of vulnerability arise. I walked faster, hoping the sensations would disappear, but of course they didn't. "Angelique, stop this," I heard my inner voice saying. I slowed my pace and allowed everything to bubble up, and with that I began to sob.

I did not wipe away my tears as I looked up to the sky. There was one star closest to the moon, which was shining so bright. My eyes fixated on it. As it shined high above the cloudless sky, it was as if it shined deep within me. It showed me how much I claimed to be responsible for other people's life events. I had been carrying a loaded bag of other people's issues and slapped an ownership label onto it for years. I started listing all the events I was not responsible for and my previous fatigue turned into an awakened energy.

Mysteries Revealed

After going through these flashbacks, I began to once again merge with the present. I somehow managed to direct my car to the shoulder of the highway. My car had stopped moving, but now my body was moving. I was trembling uncontrollably. I felt cold, afraid and in disbelief. Mentally I was telling myself that I am safe and I resorted to following my breath. I breathed in deeply as if I may not be able to take another breath. I felt charged with energy, which I was trying to redirect, but nothing seemed to be flowing through. It felt as if parts of my body were shut down, but I kept breathing because in that moment that is all I was capable of doing. It turned out to be enough.

I replayed the experience over in my mind: the driver is in front of me; I am on a highway. The car in front starts to exit off the highway and then decides to merge back onto the highway in front of me. We collide and the impact forces me into the lane to the left of me. I tightly squeeze the steering wheel and breathe in while an 18-wheeler truck hits my left side. I breathe out and I am ejected quickly back into my original lane where I am hit again.

Then the flood of questions entered my mind. How did I get to the shoulder of the highway? I can remember my breath, but I cannot recall how I got to safety. It is strange how the brain works. I found myself pondering how I could collide with a truck on a major highway and still be alive. I eventually decided to stop analyzing the whys and why nots.

My car had major damages, so I was not able to drive it. I knew I had to use the rental car and drive against my body's protest. My body was very much against the idea of driving again and it yelled, "Woman do not go behind that wheel!" I knew I had to overcome the urge of avoidance and just trust it would become easier.

On the seventh day after this unforgettable experience, I was faced with another unforgettable moment. I learned I was pregnant. A new meaning emerged and deepened my belief that the universe is extremely intentional. All things happen for a reason, even the ones which initially appear unfortunate. I did not die that evening and I will not live my life as if I am dead. Part of my life journey was to experience the beauty and blessing of motherhood.

Months passed since the car accident. Despite the neck, shoulder, back, ankle and hip pain from the collision, I felt blessed. There was not a day that passed that I did not speak with the little person growing within me. The constant pain reminded me of the collision, which deepened my gratitude for the pregnancy even more. Have you ever loved something so much you are confused about where all the love comes from? That is what it felt like when I was pregnant. I felt light, inspired and the energy growing within me. I kept up with my yoga and meditation as I felt even more connected to my baby, who was growing as much as I was. I knew that I had to move with and through all that I was feeling.

Test the waters

"You can't cross the sea merely by standing and staring at the water." – Rabindranath Tagore

Years later I handed in my resignation from what many would consider a "cushy" job, as it had great perks, financial "security" and a Montessori school close to the office. I found being in this leadership position very isolating. I was so removed from directly serving others and started to feel lost. This then led me to start feeling as if I was in fact losing my direction. There was a spiritual disconnect with my life's work and resentment started to grow. I love the field of mental and emotional health; it gives me joy to help others and show them how life can be different. I value deep connections with others and wanted to help write people's life goals with them, not write reports. I yearned to help support life transformations, not corporate initiatives.

Despite how unhappy I was, I remained at the job even when I noticed it was not serving me well. I ended up having to I take a stress leave. I remember how self-stigma trickled in as I was judging myself for not being able to keep going.

I was filled with guilt for needing to take a pause. Good old reliable guilt was always eager to show up for me. I remember trying to convince myself that I am not allowed to have emotional challenges. How can I expect others to trust what I have to offer therapeutically if I allow my stress to "get out of hand"? It reminded me of when a person tries to hold downward facing dog or chair pose in yoga with their joints not aligned; I would notice the struggle. Alignment allows things to flow more freely and this role and the new management was not in alignment with what I needed. So, the struggle began.

In retrospect, I lovingly laugh at myself, since it perplexes me how I can encourage and advocate self-compassion in others, but not for myself. It took this experience for me to become aware that I would not bestow on myself the same grace and love I would on other people. I was doing it again: trying to resist feelings and falsely believing I will gain more control of the situation if I stop doing certain things. I became the empathetic superwoman without the cape.

Eventually, I mustered up the courage to hand in my resignation and let go of all the comforts and conveniences the job offered. This led me to a new job, which required a commute into the city. Attempting to be optimistic, I viewed the long commute on the train as "me-time" and even though the commute itself was tolerable, other aspects of the job were not. Every day I would run across the parking lot with a briefcase and aggravate my back pain, all in an attempt to not miss the train. The worst thing was I had reduced time with my daughter in the mornings and in the evenings. This was not sustainable and not how I wanted to live my life. "This cannot be my calling," I remember telling myself multiple times a day. The work environment and processes of this new job were robotic and rigid. I knew very quickly it was not a healthy fit for me, but my fear of leaving another job overpowered my mind. So I remained there, feeling miserable and stuck.

One morning, I felt a warm, small knee in my ribs as my daughter tried to stretch beside me in bed. I slowly repositioned myself to see if I could get comfortable again to sleep for another 15 minutes. A few seconds passed. "Mama," she whispered. I surrendered to knowing that my sleep had come to an end and she was not going to fall back off to sleep. As we were snuggling in bed, she asked me several questions about random topics, until she stopped and made a statement instead.

"Mama," she said looking up at me and fidgeting in the bed.

"Yes, Bubs?" I answered.

As she continued to look at me with her gorgeous, captivating brown eyes, she said the words, "You need to find a job which is more slow." She snuggled closer into me as if she wanted to return to the womb, as if trying to feel through our skin-to-skin contact how I felt about her suggestion. Those words hit me right in the centre of my sternum; my stomach felt stretched and my forehead tightened. I was so embarrassed. There I was thinking I was at least doing a good job in masking how awful and fragmented I was feeling, only to find out my daughter could see through it all. I was not practicing what I preached as I had reduced my self-care practices in my life. She was right: something did need to slow down, but it was my way of being which needed to be slower, not the job.

That same day I started to visualize myself no longer in that job and opened myself up to a situation which would be better for me and those I serve. I started to surround myself with motivational words by reading new books again. It was something I always found to be helpful but had stopped making time for it. I practiced my affirming breath while on the train and stopped doing things on autopilot and started to be in the moment more. I completely revamped my self-care strategies to prepare myself for leaving that job. I made every attempt to communicate accurately with the God of the universe what I was ready to embrace and accept. Then it happened. That morning was the moment of truth — I was let go. When I was called into the HR office and heard the words, I was fascinated.

If I did not feel it within my own body, I would most likely not have completely believed it was possible. This is supposed to be a traumatic experience, so why is it that my shoulders softened down my back, my chest relaxed allowing my breath to flow easily through my body, and my jaw felt a release? It was such a profound confirmation that this was meant to happen. I felt liberated and I truly felt as if they let me go to be free. I was free to do what I was meant to do; this was how my wellness business Nurturing Our Wellbeing was born.

I walked down the path to my home with my back erect. I felt so light. I turned the key to the front door and noticed the silence within. I was washing my hands and I noticed I was smiling. I had a burst of energy that was sparking from underneath my bellybutton and it started to spread throughout my entire upper body. That very same day, instead of popping on the computer to send out my resume or CV, I started writing my vision for my emotional wellness business.

Reflective Insights

Wave of Change

I hope you can appreciate that I could not share my entire life with you within these few pages, but I am filled with gratitude that you choose to connect with me at some level as you read through some of my journey. What I hope you take away from my story is that change and evolution comes from wading through various forms of discomfort. Much like the continuous movement of the ocean, thoughts, experiences and emotions flow to shape our very existence. The undercurrent is unpredictable and can be dangerous as it has the potential to unexpectedly pull objects deep within its vastness, but there is a beautiful purpose for its very existence. The more we understand the possible purpose for our emotional undercurrents, the more we can perceive its power. Of course, this does not mean that we should jump for joy when we have a painful experience. However, we can learn from it, using it possibly to take us in a new direction. It's useful even it simply serves to teach us the act of patience and sitting with the discomfort.

I believe I will always encounter life obstacles, which I will need to either flow over, around or mindfully roll into until I can create a path through it. Loss, physical pain, witnessing injustice, embracing guilt, feeling invaded, and accepting the unexpected are all moments which required me to explore a deeper part of myself. It required me to transform. It is these very transformations which brought me to right here, right now.

Wave of Fear

Facing fear is a battle we will all encounter, but how we face it will differ. My fear for feeling certain emotions caused me to suffer longer than I needed to in many respects. Yoga placed me in a space of harmony, since it was through moving my body I was able to still my mind and heart enough to let things flow through me. In a way, my ability to embrace yoga helped me to stare fear straight in the face and I saw a reflection of my true self. Yoga is often understood as the yoke of union — a conscious connection. However, in my situation, it also offered the element of breaking down my resistance to many things, which would often block this connection. Once I became more aware of these things, the union occurred; the more I practiced, the more it revealed.

How do you gracefully identify your fears? How do you learn from your fears? When you find yourself resisting it, what fear is revealing itself?

Waves of Connection

It is essential to have a deep love for self and a connection with the people and environment which surrounds you. It is through these connections I was able to appreciate the undercurrent lying beneath all of my life experiences. Maybe you had a similar experience of awe when looking out onto a body of water. Maybe you had a moment where you stopped and looked up at the night sky and was filled with gratitude. Or maybe you watched your sleeping child and it was as if you were in a trance as you studied their beauty. These are all connections which move me to tears of joy.

I hope this encourages you to find your way to deeply connect with your life, the God of the Universe, and the beautiful spirits that surround you each and every day. I believe we all yearn for connection; it is one of the roots to our existence which adds meaning, purpose and hope. The busy flow in our society pulls us away from these things, but if we pay attention we can feel the undertow and the direction it wants to go. The waves will keep coming, that is for certain. So, my question to you is, how will you honour your undercurrents? Find your way to embrace the salty pulse of your very existence.

I am vast and have unimaginable depth. I shimmer with beauty and I reflect this beauty back into the world. We all do this in our own way. So, I send light and love your way as you take courage to flow and embrace your undercurrents just as God intended.

Breathe Deeply

CHAPTER 13

Dreams That Awaken

I AM Joan Samuels-Dennis

In 2006, I reached the peak of my seeking. Education was the vehicle by which I sought to find that thing I could not name. I was in the midst of completing the second semester of my PH.D program, and though I should have been happy, I found myself struggling with the workload intensity, the huge gap between my personal beliefs and the philosophies that guided the program, and the shifts that were occurring in key relationships as my network transformed. To say I felt misaligned with who I was and my true path would be a gross understatement.

In the midst of this struggle, I had a dream that terrified me. There are some dreams we cannot ignore. These dreams deliver a divine message and the answer to a question we are not consciously aware we are asking. They open the door to our spiritual awakening and make plain the moment we make the death wish. This dream would teach me so much about my spiritual journey and the people I would come to forgive.

"Hello Joan? It's Kim"

"Hello Kim, how are you?" I look at the clock to make sure I am not behind in getting to our appointment. But it's still early and we aren't scheduled to meet for a few hours.

"Joan, I'm sorry but an urgent matter has come up and I must deal with it as soon as possible." She sounds anxious and frazzled. Before I could get a word in, she continues, "I knew you would be disappointed, so I called the owner of the property and asked her if she could show you around. She was more than fine with that, so you are all set to go."

"Oh," I pause, trying to hide my disappointment. This is not okay, but words altogether different from what I feel leave my mouth: "I guess that should be okay."

"Joan, I know you will love this house and I can't wait for you to tell me all about it!" She quickly says goodbye.

Shift.

We drive slowly along a long winding dirt road until we come to a driveway with a signpost made from barn boards that reads "Welcome to the Matson Estates." I squeeze Richard's arm.

The path to the house is narrow, but allows us to walk side by side. Though the trees and overgrown bushes surrounding us hide a clear view of the house, we are still able to see its glistening rooftop in the distance. I draw close to Richard and we continue up the path arm in arm.

We come to a point on the path where the undergrowth parts and finally gives way to a splendid view of a stone house set on a hill. It looks as if God himself has placed it there, protected by a circle of tall trees. It glows as though the sun is frozen in place behind it. The dark brown front door with a heavy knocker is flanked by stone columns, the work of a master craftsman. It seems so familiar. I am home.

I do not immediately notice a woman is present. She is a black woman, dark in complexion, who possesses a distinction and elegance comparable to the house. She is wearing a white nurse's uniform with a light-yellow cardigan.

"You must be Richard and Joan." She says with a warm smile, "I am sorry about this, but I have been called into work. I won't be able to show you the house, but I have left the door open for you, so feel free to take your time and look around the place." The woman immediately begins walking down the trail toward the road. As we watch her, she turns and says, "My brother lives in the basement and he is a very messy person. Usually I would have cleaned up, but I did not get a chance to do so. Take a look around the upstairs, but don't go down into the basement." Then she is gone.

I am sure we went into the house. I am sure we met the Basement Dweller. Something happened there, but the dream did not reveal it to me.

Shift.

I am lost and have been for some time. I walk a deserted, moonlit dirt path alone in the dead of night, with thick forest on both sides. In the forest are people I now call Onlookers. They watch me intently with sinister and mocking eyes that glow like dim candles. I feel overwhelmed by their numbers. Why are they watching? Why don't they offer to help me?

I see a figure on the path well ahead of me. "Hello?" I can barely muster the energy but I begin to run towards it. There is a bend up ahead and I am determined not to lose him or her. Why doesn't he/she hear me? Why doesn't he/she stop and wait for me?

"Mister! Lady!" No response. The person continues walking as though unaware of my presence. The moonlight helps me to see her clearly now. I have almost caught up to her. She is a tall, slender woman with black hair that flows just below her shoulders. She wears a yellow scarf. She wears a beautiful pair of white sandals. I am so close. Why can't she at least feel my presence?

"Lady, please!" As I reach out to touch her shoulder, she fades like a vapour and disappears in the wind. Shock and utter disappointment consume me. I am alone except for the eyes in the darkness of the trees.

The elusive figure appears again and again, each time disappearing as soon as I am close enough to reach out and touch her. As the days, months, and years pass the words "Why won't anybody help me?" become the chorus of the song I sing to myself. I am tired, lost, hopeless and afraid.

As she disappears one last time, I bend with exhaustion and an uncontrollable wail erupts from the deepest part of my heart and enters the darkness surrounding me. It sinks deep into the earth and rebounds into the heavens. For a moment, the eyes in the darkness of the trees shrink back.

Shift.

I am suddenly in a new place. The trees of the forest bow toward one another and intertwine their branches to create a cave-like atmosphere. Fallen leaves lie like blankets on the ground. In the middle of this scene, Jesus sits on a fallen tree as though he has been waiting for me for some time. He wears a gown that shines white like the full moon. His face is hidden from me, but I know Him. A fire gives light and warmth. He has prepared a meal for me and though he utters no words, he tells me to eat and drink.

"I am so tired."

He says nothing but I feel his overwhelming compassion.

"I have been running for so long. I just need to rest."

Without words, I experience grace and mercy.

"They watch me." I look out in search of the eyes in the darkness. Only stillness.

"Go to sleep and I will watch over you." His voice is kind, melodious and comforting.

"You will be here when I wake up? You will not leave?" Even as I ask, I trust him completely.

"I will not leave you. I will watch over you." He is communicating without speaking.

For the first time in forever, the gaze of the Onlookers is kept out. I sleep.

From within my dream I am awoken.

"Wake up Joan." I am awoken by the gentle voice of the One who watches over me.

"I am here to tell you something." He cares for me.

"I am here to tell you that you died here many years ago." Before I even have time to ask what he means, he shows me images of my death. It is a dark, violent death. My encounter with the Basement Dweller is revealed.

Everything makes sense now.

"On the anniversary of your death, Richard parks his car in the same spot by the road and he waits for you."

New images are released. Richard is leaning against an old rusted SUV. His grief has aged him. The path for my return to him is now clear.

"Go to him. Do not stop. Run!"

I see Richard in the distance and I know where I am going. I run to unite with the one who waited for me.

Suddenly I wake.

It's been 14 years since I had that dream, yet I recall it like it happened last night. Years later, I still find depth in it. It tells the story of my spiritual death—the very moment I disconnected from myself, all others and God. This dream, along with my eventual understanding of the players in my life, set the stage for my own spiritual awakening.

We walk our path with others, who unbeknownst to us, play a significant role in our seeking and spiritual awakening.

My dream and its many characters woven into the intricate fabric of this dream offered me some metaphors for the kinds of people we encounter and forgive as we move through this life. The Realtor, Home Owner, Basement Dweller, Onlooker, Elusive Figure and Soul Lover will show themselves at various times in our lives, inspiring loving connection or fearful separation. Some play a rather minor role, but every encounter is essential for the journey and the development of our living testimony.

The **Realtor**, as an able and capable individual, is symbolic in my dream of a guide, parent, mentor, counsellor and procurer of *Living Love*. They possess both the wisdom and knowledge that can be relied upon when making important decisions about life and living. With the best of intentions, these individuals set the stage for something wonderful to enter our lives, but at the last minute something urgent captures their immediate and full attention. They exit the scene quickly, leaving us to navigate on our own a system we do not know or understand. Even worse, they reassign us to someone who is ill-prepared and incapable of bringing our plans to completion.

From this character, we want an enduring faithfulness, commitment, devotion, sustained and prioritized interest, and calm. Instead, the Realtor enters and leaves our lives never knowing the chain reaction they have initiated. They inspire feelings of abandonment, neglect, insignificance, and betrayal.

The **Home Owner**, a warm and seemingly refined individual, is symbolic in my dream of a care taker, guardian, family member, teacher, religious leader or authority figure. They appear to possess the very thing we seek. They take on the role of the Realtor not because they are able to do so, but rather because they genuinely desire to keep the door open to satisfying the need for a fruitful exchange. Though they are warm and caring, we know little about them, except that they are willing to relinquish the thing that we desire to possess. They too have priorities that cause them to exit the scene quickly, leaving us to find our own way. Beyond this, hidden and unresolved issues from their past and present expose us to an environment that is likely to throw us off course or harm us. Our protection, if addressed, will likely be an afterthought or something they gingerly bring to our attention.

From this character we want truth, integrity, readiness, transparency and protection. Instead, the Home Owner leaves unexpectedly, neglects the messy state of their environment, and neglectfully exposes us to a great violation. They inspire feelings of shock, confusion, wonder, anxiety, despair, and betrayal.

The **Basement Dweller,** lives stuck in an emotional and spiritual state that can only be described as toxic. In my dream, they are symbolic of any individual, group, institution or human system that succumbs to the Spirit of Fear. They inflict wounds that birth within us anxiety, despair, grief, loneliness, isolation, doubt, weariness, failure, oppression, bitterness, jealousy, unforgiveness and spiritual poverty. Our encounter with the Basement

Dweller brings a state of spiritual death, a tomb that for a time separates us from ourselves, all others and God.

They introduce into our life a struggle so challenging only isolation allows us to endure it. Like an animal overcome by a predator, we fain death, shut down, and choose to die. We say out loud, "This is all too much. If this is what life is like, I choose not to live it." We engage in a life pattern that fulfills the death wish. Without a conscious awareness, we birth the false self — the *wounded* self — and the self that develop fear-based *attachments* to people, places and situations that bring us a false sense of safety. Alternatively, we also develop fear-based *aversions* to people, places and situations that mirror the circumstance in which we were wounded.

From this character we want freedom, peace, rest, and fearless living. Instead, the Basement Dweller brings conflict and war, kills our hopes and dreams and steals our joy. They pour into our cup a toxic brew of spiritual darkness and chaos. They cross lines no human should ever cross. They kill us. They inspire fear. Our encounter with the Basement Dweller is the place from which we must all choose to rise and begin our spiritual transformation journey.

The **Onlooker** is symbolic in my dream of the people around us who do nothing, even when witnessing the deeds of the Basement Dweller or our struggle in the aftermath. They are family members, friends, co-workers and Sunday school teachers who themselves have their own struggle with the Spirit of Fear. Their ominous curiosity, silence and grotesque inaction are what makes them dangerous. They watch our struggles unmoved, staying in the shadows, neither celebrating our overcoming nor helping during times of great need.

They will convince you that you are foolish for taking up the charge against injustice. As thoughts of action overwhelm them, they will say with a loud voice:

"Why do you speak about such things?"

"The fight is too big!"

"There is so much evil!"

"Am I my brother's keeper?"

"Making this world better is impossible!"

"If it is His will, let God do it!"

From this character we want empathy, compassion, understanding, courage, and just and merciful action. Instead, the Onlooker is overcome with fear and watches silently. Rendered powerless by the scene before them and their own struggles, they are ill-prepared to help and at times are indifferent to the path we walk. They inspire feelings of loneliness and isolation.

The **Elusive Figure**, is symbolic in my dream of the true self or the spiritual self. Many of us spend a lifetime chasing the Elusive Figure. For a time, we look outward, believing that the happiness that comes with our reconnection to our true self can be found in romantic relationships, education, career, wealth, status, professional partnerships, personal aspirations and achievement. The chase ends when we stop looking outward and instead begin our spiritual quest to find the true self within. We must reconcile with the Elusive Figure before we can reconcile with the Holy Spirit. Reconciliation with the true self and the Holy Spirit reveals the deep desires of the spiritual heart. It reveals our power to give ourselves that very thing we have been asking others to give us.

From this character we want presence, recognition, acknowledgment, guidance, stability and oneness. Instead, the Elusive Figure is seemingly deaf, blind, insensitive, inattentive, ignorant and alarmingly mysterious. It is the separation from the true self that inspires and maintains fear.

The **Soul Lover** is symbolic in my dream of the people who love us and desire our healing and the return of the true self. They are husbands, wives, sisters, brothers, friends and other significant figures that witness the moments that bring us to our knees. They bear witness to huge waves of despair, grief and anger that crash over us, believing we possess both the strength and resilience needed to pull ourselves back to the surface. They wait for as long as it takes for us to heal and embrace our true identity. Though they struggle with us and make demands for our return, they persevere with faith and hope that one day we will shed the pain and return to them and to ourselves.

From this character we want enduring and unending hope. Though the Soul Lover grieves for us, it is their hope that empowers us to rise from the dead.

Every relationship formed with another is entered into with expectations of experiencing *Living Love*. What we get instead is fear. Encounters with the Realtor, Home Owner, Basement Dweller, Onlooker, Elusive Figure, and Soul Lover cannot and do not give us all that we seek, but they ready us for a more beautiful encounter, an encounter with the all-consuming and unconditional love that can only be described with one word: God.

From God we want Divine protection and an escape from all that is terrifying in this human existence. Instead, the Good Sheppard is seemingly silent, invisible, distant and untouchable. Eventually, as the fog of unforgiveness and fear lifts, we understand that the Holy Spirit has always been present, awaiting our call for help.

The house we seek is living love, a Divine sanctuary possessing an unending beauty that escapes the human mind. It is the living and breathing embodiment of joy, peace and hope. A house built on the strong foundation of a Divine, compassionate love that purifies the heart and enlightens the spirit. Its walls are strong with a patience that endures all worldly concerns and the frailties of humanity. The protective wisdom of its many rooms offers rest, even as we wonder at the amazing grace and mercy woven into the fabric of its furnishings. It shelters and transforms us as we seek refuge from life's great storms. Its goodness keeps at bay all that is evil.

Ultimately, we must all understand this truth: *Living Love* is already ours, but only a state of stillness allows the love that radiates from the Creator to permeate our heart, soul and mind. The God of the Universe knows our needs before we cry for help. He offers a meeting place of comfort to the weary, companionship to the lost, food for the hungry, safety and security for the oppressed, and a soft place to lay down and rest at the moment we request it.

When we are ready, the Holy One opens our eyes to memories of the past, present and future that are essential for rising and becoming beautiful I am. God illuminates the sources of our suffering and spiritual death, and bears witness as we rise and are firmly replanted in a place of love and peace. The old, tired self becomes new again, enlightened with the gifts granted to us before we entered this human frame. For the remainder of the journey, the Holy Spirit is our guide, and His voice is the map by which we enter he village of peace.

CHAPTER 14

Christ-Like Forgiveness

I AM Joan Samuels-Dennis

Christ is the only Divine Avatar of forgiveness, and it is His kind of forgiveness that spiritually awakens, renews, restores and establishes new spiritual patterns that foster health in the heart, mind and soul. In her book *The Body Remembers: A Conscious Choice to Live* (1994), Kandis Blakely designed a forgiveness process called "New Decision Therapy." She identified seven steps in the process.

The first four steps address a series of questions that bring clarity about the thing we want from every person we encounter and eventually forgive. The last three steps address a series of declarations we must make that release the record of wrongs, revoke the death wish and embrace fearless living. The questions are simple and remain unchanged because they transcend age, sex, race, culture, social status, geographic location and even spiritual orientation.

Since discovering the technique, I have altered the declarations and the spiritual foundation on which they sit. I have oriented them within a framework I call *Christ-Like Forgiveness*.

Forgiveness is a process that purifies and transforms the heart, soul and mind. It exposes knowledge, wisdom and lessons designed specifically for living a life filled with love and purpose. Forgiveness allows us to clearly see the connection between our most painful moments and God's plan and purpose for our lives. It allows us to step into a place of purity and balance. Forgiveness is the path to love and enlightenment.

Each act of forgiveness requires that we reflect on the thing we want and this is achieved with two questions:

1. *What did you want from the person that they were not able, capable, or ready to give you?*

2. *What did you get instead?*

As we move through the forgiveness process, we gain access to three pieces of information we all must know if we are to love and live fearlessly: our love language, our fear trigger, and our fear language.

What do we all want from every encounter with another? The simple answer is we all want *love*. The truth is, it is already ours. The multiple moments in which we are wounded and especially our encounter with the Basement Dweller, creates the false belief as we say out loud "my source of love is gone!" We follow that with other statements: I am not good. I am not good enough. I am not worthy of love. We lose our peace and despair erupts as we wonder about what we did to deserve the violent acts of separation and disconnection.

Looking across all acts of forgiveness, we begin to notice a pattern. Each forgiveness reveals a list of wants or spiritual desires that when combined allows us to speak our love language—the unique way we desire to give and receive love. There are variations in how we define love, but each of us is seeking compassion, gracious favour that is unconditional, patience, kindness, commitment, truth and faithfulness. This perfect love we desire is possessed only by God. It is only when we overcome the fears birthed in the moments of wounding that we realize the love we seek has always been present.

What do each of us get instead of love? The simple answer is we all get fear. Our fears will show themselves in obvious and discrete ways. The child conceived by rape will fear force and violation. The adopted child will fear separation and rejection. The child who experiences domestic violence will fear male authority. The seven-year-old who is laughed at by her classmates will fear judgement. The young woman who is raped will fear vulnerability and the very presence of God.

As we continue to move through the forgiveness process, we are asked to contemplate our response to fear with this question:

How did it make you feel when you got what you got instead of what you wanted?

When we forgive, it is important that we connect deeply with our emotions. The visualizations embedded in the forgiveness process allows us to re-enter the scene as an observer. It allows us to look intently at our self as well as the people in the room and honestly express how "getting what we got" impacted us physically, emotionally and spiritually. When we own our feelings, it is then that we develop the capacity to respond to the Spirit of Fear with power, clarity of mind and self-control.

Each act of forgiveness enhances our emotional intelligence by helping us to become consciously aware of our physical responses even before the corresponding emotional responses can be fully expressed. In his book *Life Energy: Using the Meridians to Unlock the Hidden Power of Your Emotions* (1985), Dr. John Diamond combined his knowledge of Western and traditional Chinese medicine to help us understand the emotions we experience and how they link to the 12 vital organs of the body. Presented below are two tables outlining the emotions associated with the states of love and fear.

Table 1: Emotions Associated with the State of Love

Meridian	State of Love
Lung	Humility, Tolerance, Modesty
Liver	Happiness, Cheer
Gall Bladder	Connection, Love, Adoration
Spleen	Faith and Confidence about the future, Security
Kidney	Sexual assuredness, Identity Assuredness
Large Intestine	Worthiness
Circulatory and Reproductive organs	Letting Go of the Past, Generosity and Relaxation
Heart	Love, Forgiveness
Stomach	Contentment, and Tranquillity
Thyroid	Hope, Light, Resilience, and Elation
Small Intestine	Joy
Bladder	Peace, Harmony, Patience, Calm

Table 2: Emotions Associated with the State of Fear

Meridian	State of Fear
Lung	Disdain, Scorn, Contempt, Intolerance, Haughtiness, False pride, Prejudice
Liver	Unhappiness
Gall Bladder	Rage, Fury, Wrath
Spleen	Realistic Anxiety About the Future
Kidney	Sexual Indecision, Identity Insecurity
Large Intestine	Guilt, Shame
Circulatory and Reproductive organs	Jealousy, Sexual Tension, Regret, Remorse, Stubbornness
Heart	Anger
Stomach	Disappointment, Disgust, Bitterness, Greed, Emptiness, Deprivation, Nausea, Hunger
Thyroid	Depression, Despair, Grief, Hopelessness, Oppression, Dejection, Loneliness, Isolation
Small Intestine	Sadness, Sorrow
Bladder	Restlessness, Impatience, Frustration

As we move through each act of forgiveness and recall the things said and the actions taken, we have an automatic body-mind-spirit response that is easy to miss unless we become intentionally mindful of it. A tingle or burst of energy indicates a positive or loving emotional response, while a pinch, pin prick or uncomfortable sensation implies a negative or fearful emotional response. Once we know the location of each meridian point, Dr. Diamond's work can be used to help us decipher with great precision the emotions that come forward as we move through the forgiveness process.

A successful forgiveness hinges on our capacity to dive deep, speak truth, empathize and offer Christ-like compassionate understanding to the one who wronged us. This requires that we reflect on a fourth question:

What circumstance(s) caused the person(s) to behave as they did?

Compassionate understanding requires that each of us step into the other person's shoes and gain a new level of awareness of the myriad internal and external factors that influenced their capacity to love and remain in a place of trust, faith and hope. We see with a new level of clarity that our battle is not with our spiritual brother or sister, nor our neighbours, but with the Spirit of Fear — a spiritual entity established among the generations who lived before us. As we embrace this Christ-like compassion, we begin to see things from God's perspective, and we give up altogether the judgement, blaming, shaming, abandonment, neglect and punishment of the other. We stand instead in a place of neutral observation as we grab hold of the understanding that we are cups constantly being filled with fear or love, and that we give what has been given to us in the measure it was given.

As we grow in our capacity to have compassion for the other, we also grow in our capacity to have compassion for our self. Our sense of power expands and we begin to desire what God desires for all of us—reconnection and reconciliation. A new awareness comes as we realize that we do not break the patterns of separation and disconnection with human strength. Instead, God's Holy Spirit empowers us to do it.

God felt humanity's disconnection in the Garden and immediately made plans for a choice-filled reconnection. God also feels our spiritual disconnection when we make the death wish. Christ represents the word of God's heart. When Jesus went to the cross, he created a path for our return. When we forgive and choose to "let go," we join God in expressing the word of our heart to let go of the wrong and reconnect with the one who harmed us. The first declaration in the forgiveness process goes something like this:

"I let go of the anger, guilt, regret . . . I have towards you for . . ."

It's a very simple statement but it has so much power. We let go of the fear — the thing we got. We let go of the fear response — the feelings, ill-formed beliefs, toxic thoughts and impulsive, uncontrolled behaviours. We tip our cup and pour out the thing that was poured into us. Then we look up and ask God to replace it with love. We breathe deeply and we repeat the declaration once more:

"Just like Christ, I let go. It is finished."

As we "let go" and release the other, we mirror Christ and say, "It is finished!" With that, we fling the door wide open for the light and love of the Holy Spirit to enter. We become filled with a spirit of love, power, and clarity of mind. Every forgiveness brings forward once hidden insights, wisdom and revelations that allow us to make yet another declaration:

"I love you and accept you for who you are . . . where you are . . . and the beautiful spirit you will become."

When we can say, "I love you," we are choosing to recognize with all humility that we are all children of a loving God. As members of a human nation, you are my bother and you are my sister. Furthermore, as members of a spiritual nation, we are ONE. This statement allows us to shed the lie that love is conditional. We shed the spiritual lies told for generations. We finally see ourselves authentically for who we are: Children of a loving God who sees us as good enough to die for. Are we perfect? No, of course not. But we are good enough.

It is not in our own strength that we love completely and without conditions. When God's spirit abides with us, godliness and goodness become a possibility. Beyond this the Holy Spirit gives us the strength to continually think on things that are true, honourable, worthy of respect, pure and wholesome. We think on things that bring peace. We seek the gift of love and as we seek, this most excellent gift is granted to us.

In this life, we are to become like Christ [1 John 4:17, AMP]. We are to forgive and live fearlessly. Every organ in our body should light up like a city on a hill, bringing out the God-colours in the world [Matthew 5:14-16 MSG]. Fearless living allows us to deeply connect with God. Christ is the path through which we reconnect and reconcile with love. Christ-like forgiveness allows each of us to spiritually awaken to the "good" creation that we are and to the "goodness" of our Creator.

Forgiveness reminds us that Christ did not remain in the tomb. He rose from the dead and sits at the right hand of God, the Good Father. Beyond this, He possesses a spiritual authority that restrains the Spirit of Fear and renders it powerless. As we make a new decision to pursue love and not the patterns that give life to fear, we must also choose to rise and exit our tomb. It is here we make the choice to trust, hope and have faith in the One who died for us. It is here that we undo the death wish. We shout from the mountaintop a final declaration:

"I choose to live, not die!"
"I choose to rise and move on with my life!"
"I choose to be happy and healthy!"
"I choose to live fully energized and walking in step with my purpose!"
"I choose to be like Christ!"
"I will forgive!"
"I will love."
"I will reconcile!"
"I choose peace!"

This is quite the declaration and we cannot make it without considering what it means for our relationship with God, our self and all others. We release the old fear-led self and embrace the new love-led self. As we choose to be happy, healthy and live life fully energized, every organ in our body aligns with a state of love. We experience spiritual balance and our eyes glow, showing evidence of the light that dwells within.

Our purpose is to love. Christ-like forgiveness is the embodiment of love!

ACKNOWLEDGMENTS

Becoming

I am excited about the start of a new decade. I call 2020 the decade of awakening and the period in time God has elected to bring the new age of peace. It is the decade during which those who are ready will be transformed and emerge from their cocoons as the beautiful butterfly.

In October 2016, I attended a book-writing conference, and there the idea for this book project Becoming: The Journey to Love was created. I spoke to my new-found friend and business partner about writing a book that told the stories of black women. We were both very excited, but as we talked about the book and its intentions, it became clear that the book could not be just about black women. No, this book would be about women's struggles, their pain and the journey of overcoming. This book would be about our rise to that beautiful place called the village of peace.

I became a resident of this place after moving through a spiritual transformation journey that took exactly 3 years and six months. What I can say is this, I returned to a spiritual home--a home found only in the purest part of man's heart where God's spirit resides. I live among a group of women that love God, all people, places and things. In this village, we share a perspective that this life is a human experience entered by spiritual beings. There is a knowing among us that eventually we must all choose death or go in search of peace.

For the Becoming book project, we sought out and recruited women who had struggled and arrived at an in-between space called love, and we asked them to tell their stories about how they got there. We did not realize that most stories would be about violence. Slowly, I have come to this understanding: only those enthralled in a spiritual war, are inclined to seek peace.

I am thankful for women of the Becoming Book Project for adopting the vision for this book and patiently waiting for it to come to fruition. The project took over three years to complete but, I know there is a season for everything and all things are happening exactly as they should. Thank you, dear sisters, of Becoming!

Kate Kelty is a writer and speaker who offers care and support to those who are grieving. Her professional background as a counsellor to women in crisis pregnancies, as well as Kate's first-hand experience with grief after the death of her daughter, Anna, is the foundation for

Kate's first book, The Jesus of My Grief. Kate also blogs for The Grace to Grieve and is a contributing author for TakeThemAMeal.com, a meal coordination service used by millions across the world. Kate is a mother of five, a pastor's wife and a project manager/decorator for a home builder, all in the beautiful Shenandoah Valley. Kate's great passion and purpose is to come alongside others in their pain, offering hope and understanding amid their despair.

You can hear more from Kate and obtain her book at www.TheGracetoGrieve.com

Contessa Beckford, is a woman of faith and courage. She is a scholar, writer, budding entrepreneur, and beloved mother. She has obtained a Bachelor's of Science, Masters of Public Health, and is currently completing her Doctorate in Public Health (Epidemiology).

June 2016, she followed her heart to fulfill her God-given purpose, which was to reach others through education and encouragement. Contessa and her sister Candace came together in 2016 to fulfill their purpose and life-long goal of working together, and created Sis∞Arias United.

Contessa believes that life is truly a gift that should not be taken for granted, but instead be used to bring about change and growth within our lives and the lives of those around us.

Nene Akintan's greatest passion is empowering Minority Women and Children. She uses her life story to help others overcome intense hardship and blossom. In formal and informal settings she motivates others by providing effective tools and tips, learned from her own trials and triumphs. Nene has a BSc, Sociology and Anthropology; a Master's in Business Administration and Marketing; a Master's in Science with a specialization in Management/Human Resources. She runs a foundation that empowers disadvantage children and youth in North America and Nigeria.

Rayna Hillary has been an Artist at Razzy Art since 2018. Her passion is helping people of all ages relax & enjoy Art in new way through acrylic pouring and other mediums. In addition to being an Artist she is a mother of 3 & a health enthusiast who helps individuals focus on important issues to restructure their lives to be more purposeful when it comes to the area of proper nutrition for themselves & their families.

Daniela Parlane is a wife, mother of three, blogger, author and speaker. In partnership with her husband Cassidy Parlane, she established a ministry called Make Your Marriage Great Again, a spinoff from their book "What Love Is Not". The book was birth from their strikingly similar experience of a failed marriage, and their mutual passion to help others succeed at marriage.

Her second book, "Words Of A Mute Girl" depicts her journey with a debilitating anxiety disorder that she struggled with as a child and overcame. Her great passion is to inspire others to have healthy Godly relationships. Together we organize and speak at marriage conferences, seminars, workshops and musical events. For more information, visit www.makeyourmarriagegreatagain.ca

Yolanda De Souza is an educator and creator of Empowerment — an anti-bullying program for youth and girls that addresses self-esteem, acceptance and self-awareness. She has given talks at Diversity Conferences and workshops to help influence the development of inclusive education programs. She is on a mission to help young girls embrace who they truly are and grow to be strong confident young women despite the pressures of daily life. Yolanda enjoys sharing her journey of moving past her personal struggles to obtaining personal peace, joy, and freedom.

Tatiana Lopez was born in Costa Rica. She enjoys spending time with family and friends, and especially enjoys helping others. She loves nature, hiking in the mountains, practicing meditation, reading, doing pilates, yoga and traveling around the world. She studied Political Science and earned two Master's Degree in Communication and Digital Marketing. She is currently studying Graphic Design. She likes to explore new worlds of knowledge, to grow as a human being in the spiritual, social and intellectual way. She has worked in government institutions, mass media, universities and civil society organizations in Costa Rica and Latin America.

Trisha Ollivierre reside in Grenada and is a social science graduate from T.A. Marryshow community college. She is a youth advocate and book illustrator. She serves her community as a receptionist at a local pharmacy. She finds pleasure in writing short stories, reading Christian genre and painting.

Angelique Benois has over 18 years nursing experience. She holds a degree in Psychology, a Master's of Science in Nursing and completed her Nurse Practitioner degree, specializing in mental health. In 2017, she received a Worldwide Leader in Healthcare nursing award from the International Nurses Association for her contribution to the profession.

Trained as a Yoga Instructor in Goa, India, Angelique now combines her extensive mental health clinical background with her yoga expertise through her business titled: Nurturing Our Wellbeing (N.O.W) where she offers integrated corporate wellness workshops. Angelique is a mother and one of her favorite activities is travelling the world to learn cultures and remind herself of all the possibilities the world has to offer.
www.nurturingourwellbeing.com

Marsha Miller, is an entrepreneur who prides herself on teaching financial literacy to youth and adults from economically disadvantaged communities. She an author, a poet, a motivational speaker, worship leader and evangelist who is passionate about youth and is especially inspired to reach those who have experienced trauma whether emotional, physical or sexual in nature. She is a mother to two beautiful children and very active in her community. She is the project manager for the Stem Hub Foundation, an organization that connects youth to community mentors as they also expose youth to careers in science, technology, engineering and math.

ABOUT THE EDITOR

Dr. Joan

Joan Samuels-Dennis is the director and founder of the Canadian Council for World Peace (CCWP), an independent, not-for-profit organization that works to promote the health and spiritual well-being of diverse people groups globally and strengthen the capacity of individuals, families and communities to achieve a fairer, just and peaceful world.

She holds a Doctor of Philosophy in Nursing from the University of Western Ontario with a specialization in mental health promotion. She established the CCWP in response to a deep and spiritually driven desire to see every individual transform into the most loving, powerful, and authentic beings they were born to be. She is a powerful speaker with an incredible message that inspires people to embrace their true selves as children of God, to push through moments of intense struggle, and align their lives with the Creator's plans for their life.

Dr. Joan is the author of *490: Forgive and Live Fearlessly*, a book which presents an eye-opening forgiveness process that helps men, women, and children experience a personal and spiritual transformation that moves them from that *place of stuckness* that is often mis-interpreted as mental illness, into a place where they live with passion and purpose.

Dr. Joan is the creator of the *Becoming Book Project*, an anthology written by women about their transitions from places of struggle to that place she calls *the village of peace*. Several times throughout the year, she hosts a Truth, Forgiveness and Reconciliation event that draws attention to a human rights issue affecting our most vulnerable populations. Her life's work is now dedicated to putting a spot light on the many issues faced by the African Diaspora which continues to experience the transgenerational consequences of slavery.

- 🌐 www.drjoan.ca
- 🌐 www.canadiancouncilworldpeace.ca
- ✉️ connect@drjoan.ca
- 🔗 https://www.linkedin.com/in/dr-joan-6b990146/
- Ⓐ Other books published by Dr. Joan:
  490: Forgive and Live Fearlessly on Amazon and Kindle

Made in the USA
Middletown, DE
21 March 2020